Better Homes and Gardens

All-New Edition

BEST OF Halloween
tricks & treats

A Better Homes and Gardens® Book
An Imprint of
HMH

contents

Pumpkins

Parties

Costumes

Treats

Outdoor Decor

Bonuses

save
a
eat
apple
pie!

pumpkins

Ghoulish or grinning, spooky or sparkling, witty or witchy—pumpkins set the season's tone. Whether you can't wait to get to the carving or you prefer a no-knives option, these clever characters are ready to help you express your creativity—and show off your Halloween style.

Leave 'em laughing or running for cover with this crop of ingenious jack-o'-lanterns. Requiring little to no carving, these designs use spray paint, ribbon, paper, and embellishments to make them fun, and our instructions and patterns make them easy.

PUMPKINS *with panache*

ugh! a bug!
Anything that makes your skin crawl is fun fare for Halloween. Pumpkins go to great lengths, *opposite*, to form a caterpillar that's camouflaged with adhesive-backed felt dots.

no-bake cake
This tiered confection, *above*, has all the ingredients to please a princess: lacy trims, adhesive gems, pastel "icing," and a Cinderella squash for the base.

TRICK
TREAT

all tricked out

Welcome trick-or-treaters with pumpkins that display the favorite words of the season, *opposite*. Spray paint and masking tape create the easy stripes. Paint a single word on each pumpkin, or paint "Trick" on one side and "Treat" on the other for a pumpkin that covers the Halloween choices from front to back. Add sticker dots or drill holes to complete the look.

who's next?

This ghostly pumpkin pair is bound to make heads roll, *above*. To get the haunted look—Headless Horseman–style—just add paint, lace, ribbon, and letter stickers to conjure up a mysterious madame and an ominous message to warn all of what's to come.

he's a crack-up

Perch this clumsy character of nursery rhyme fame, *opposite*, on a retaining wall or your front step and he's sure to elicit giggles from passersby. And don't worry—this Humpty Dumpty is easy to put together, thanks to a painted face, paper legs, and a funnel for a cap.

get truckin'

Big-rig pumpkins, *above*, call for hefty construction. Built from scraps of 2×4 lumber, the vehicles can be used year after year—just replace the gourds.

happy owl-oween

Who-whooo better to stand watch on All Hallows' Eve than Harry Potter's Hedwig? Our snowy version, *left*, works up like magic with just a little carving, some easy gouging, and a colorful touch of paper magic.

Perform Halloween crafts magic when you tape off the stem and transform your pumpkin with a quick coat of spray paint!

they're having a ball

These zany pumpkins, *opposite*, have an eye for the offbeat. To give them their off-kilter looks, tap into a collection of eyeball-design rubber balls and embellish them with marker-drawn details. Pair mismatched balls for a cockeyed presentation, and use paint for the pumpkins' goofy grins.

trompe l'oeil treat

Too big to pop in your mouth, these titanic "candies," *above*, still look good enough to eat. Make them using cone-shape orange pumpkins and two colors of spray paint.

Take an autumn hike and gather a few of Mother Nature's own crafts supplies: seeds, nuts, feathers, and berries.

what a hoot

Only wise owls could create pumpkins with so much personality and without any carving. With seeds for flowerlike eyes, feathers for pointy ears, and nuts for beaks, these owls, *above*, are a natural favorite. Complete the flock with mini white gourd owlets decorated with berries and tufts of feathers.

boo-rah!

Ready to raise some Halloween hackles? With a jarful of black buttons and a bottle of glue, you can give any pumpkin a ghostly shout, *opposite top.*

web crawlers
Who would guess that these little web crawlers, *right,* are actually pie pumpkins in disguise? Black glitter paint, chenille stems, and wiggly eyes spin these pumpkins into spiderlike existence.

Ugh! A Bug!

Spray-paint pumpkins apple green. Paint the stems with black crafts paint and a brush. From peel-and-stick felt, punch out the following: assorted 1-inch, 1¼-inch, and 1½-inch circles from yellow and orange for body spots; two 1½-inch circles from black and two 1¼-inch circles from white for eyes. Press circles to pumpkins, referring to the photo, *above,* for guidance.

Hot-glue a 1-inch-diameter googly eye to each felt eye. For antennae, paint two ¾-inch-diameter wood beads orange with yellow dots. Thread the beads onto two orange chenille stems; coil stems around a fat marker to shape. Drill holes into the head pumpkin and insert the antennae.

No-Bake Cake

Remove stems from a medium-size pumpkin and a large Cinderella squash. Spray-paint a small pumpkin lavender, the medium-size pumpkin pale yellow, and the large Cinderella squash pink.

For the lavender pumpkin, cut two ribbon lengths in different styles to run from the stem to the base of the pumpkin, plus ½ inch. (We used ¾-inch-wide flower-edged light green ribbon and ⅛-inch-wide pink satin ribbon.) Holding the ribbons together as a single length of trim, turn under ¼ inch at one raw edge and pin the ribbons to the top of the pumpkin using a pearl-head pin. Bring trim to the bottom of the pumpkin and pin it; repeat with additional ribbon lengths, spacing evenly, to encircle the pumpkin. Press ¼-inch-diameter adhesive pearls along each length of trim.

Arrange ⅜-inch-wide pink braid in even scallops around the top of the yellow pumpkin, pushing straight pins into the tips of the scallops to secure the braid to the pumpkin. Hot-glue small bows atop the pins. Press ¼-inch green adhesive gems onto the pumpkin below the scallops.

Drape ⅛-inch-diameter lavender satin cord over the lobes of the pink squash as shown, *below left,* alternating single and double loops and hot-gluing in place at the stem. Drape lengths of clear beaded cord between the double loops, gluing them at the stem. Using pearl-head pins, pin a plastic flower bead or silk flower inside each section of draped cord. Stack the pumpkins to form the tiered "cake."

All Tricked Out

Using masking or painter's tape, mask areas of a pumpkin to create a wide center stripe and additional stripes of differing widths. Cover the areas you want to remain the pumpkin color, including the stem. The wide center stripe should have space for "Trick," "Treat," or another Halloween word.

Spray-paint the pumpkin black; remove tape. Using your desired font, print your preferred word in a size to fit inside the wide center stripe; cut out letters using

scissors. Position the letters on the pumpkin; trace around them with a pencil. Remove letters. Trace the penciled outlines using a thin black marker. Paint inside the outlines using black crafts paint.

Create dots in black-painted areas by drilling holes with a cup drill bit. If you'd rather not drill, use circle stickers to make the dots.

Make polka-dot pumpkins by applying black circle stickers to a white pumpkin.

Who's Next?

Cut out a silhouette image and trace onto your pumpkin with a pencil. Paint the silhouette black. Spray with varnish to set the paint. Cut a length of black lace to fit in a circle around the silhouette. Pin the lace in place with pearl-head pins.

For the "Off with Your Head" pumpkin, use letter stickers to spell out the message on a white pumpkin. Use pearl-head pins to attach narrow black ribbon to the pumpkin, following the rib lines as a guide.

He's a Crack-Up

Note: See "Creative Carving Basics," page 46, for a guide to tools, tips, and techniques such as transferring patterns.

Transfer the pattern for the face, *below*, onto a pie pumpkin. Using crafts paint and a paintbrush, paint the eyes white. Paint the mouth, nose, and eye pupils black. Spray with varnish to set the paint.

Follow the instructions, *right,* to make the paper pumpkin legs. Using the pattern, *below*, cut two feet from red paper. Glue a foot to the bottom of each folded paper-chain leg. Glue the other end of each leg to the bottom of the painted pumpkin.

Place an old funnel on top of the pumpkin for a hat.

PUMPKIN LEGS

Cut 3×60-inch paper strips, two purple and two black. Lay one purple and one black strip perpendicular to each other, overlapping the pieces at one end; glue in place.

Fold the vertical strip over the horizontal strip (see diagrams, *bottom*). Fold the horizontal strip over the vertical strip. Repeat alternately folding the vertical and horizontal strips over each other. Pull the ends to open the chain.

Repeat the folding technique to make a second chain.

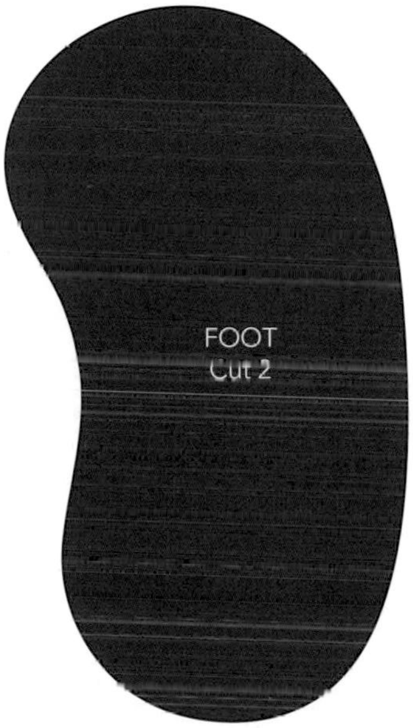

He's a Crack-Up
Enlarge to desired size.

DIAGRAMS FOR PUMPKIN LEGS

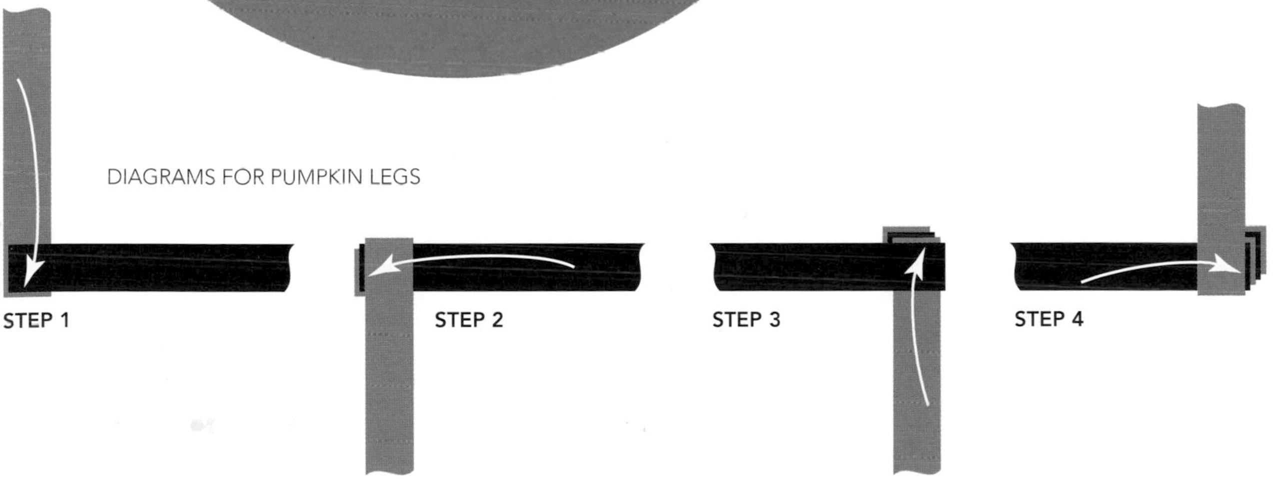

Get Truckin'

Following the Wrecking Ball Truck and Cement Mixer patterns, *below*, cut all shapes from 2×4 scrap lumber, except cut the crane from a 1×1-inch trim piece. Drill holes as noted. Assemble the wooden truck bodies using flathead wood screws. Attach wooden plug headlights using wood glue.

Spray-paint the vehicles. We used light olive and yellow.

WRECKING BALL TRUCK

Wrap the base of the truck with a strip of ¾-inch-wide black electrician's tape. Place ¾-inch-wide red electrician's tape diagonally across the black tape on each side of the truck. Trim the excess red tape with a crafts knife.

Drill a hole through the stem of a small gourd. Spray-paint the gourd silver. Fasten a clip-and-triangle ring onto one end of a 4-inch length of chain and a triangle ring onto the opposite end. Thread the triangle ring through the stem hole. Screw the clip into the top of the crane.

For each hubcap, hot-glue a ⅝-inch-diameter black button onto a ¾-inch-diameter blue button. Hot-glue a hubcap to each end of three 5- to 6-inch-long delicata squash for wheels. Set the wrecking ball truck atop the wheels.

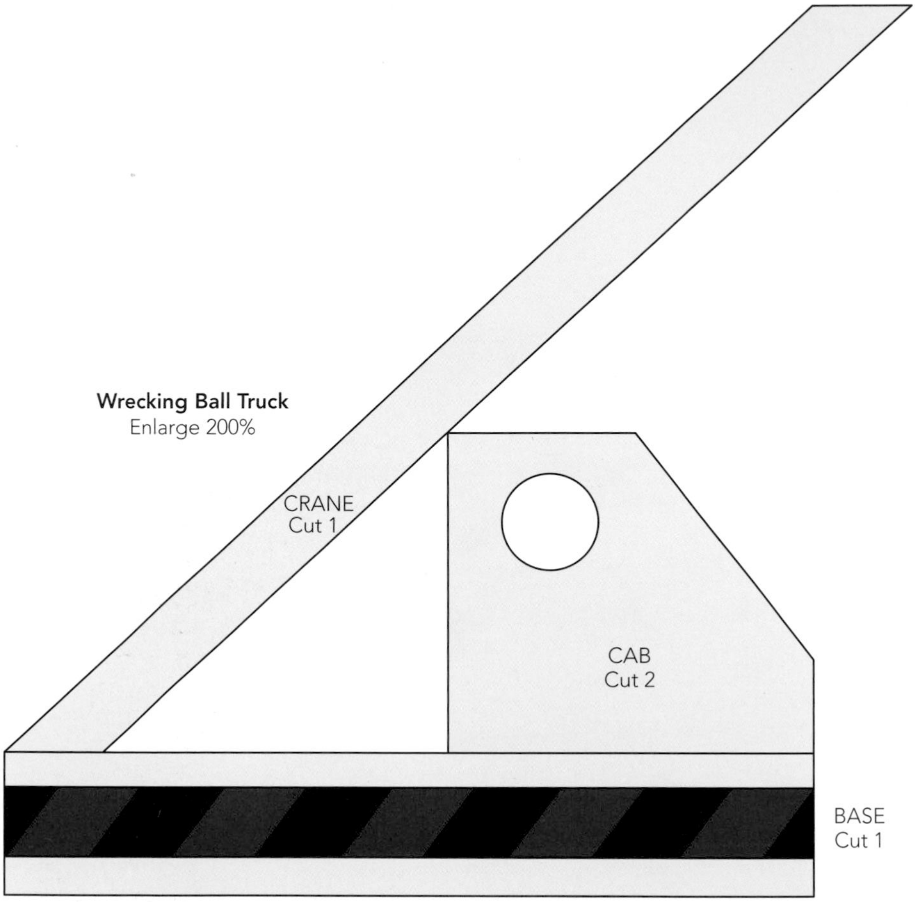

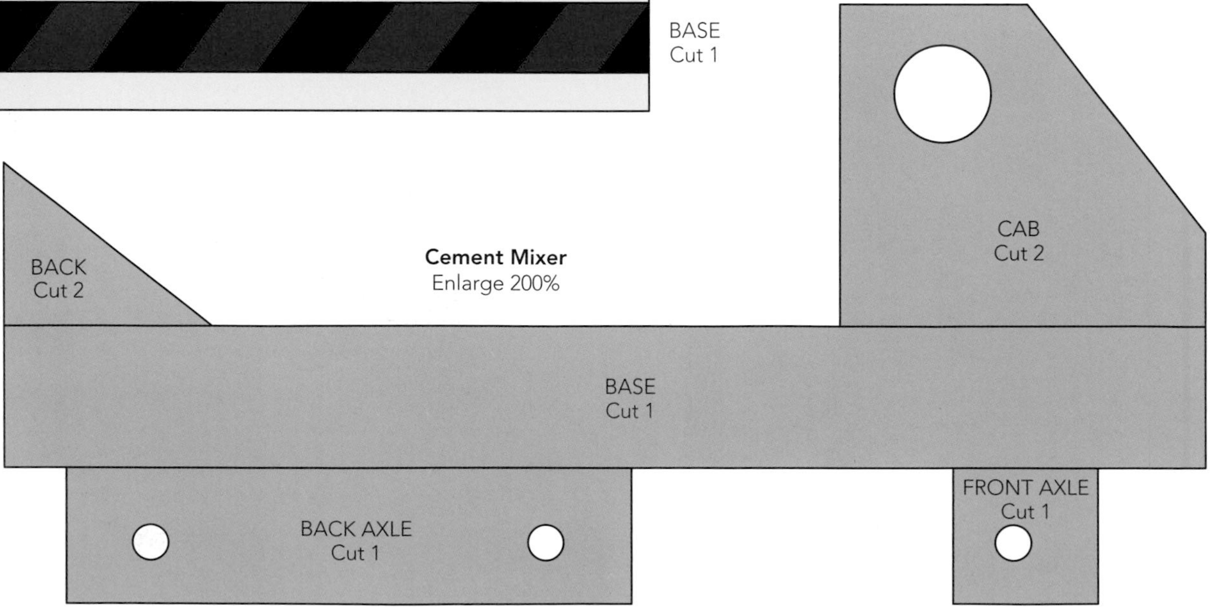

CEMENT MIXER

For wheels, choose squash or gourds with ¼-inch-diameter stems. For each hubcap, hot-glue a 1-inch orange button onto a 1¼-inch metal washer. Hot-glue washers to the bottom of each squash. Push stems into the holes in the truck base.

For the cement mixer tank, wrap a 9-inch-long spaghetti squash with ¾-inch-wide black electrician's tape. Add diagonal bands of ¾-inch-wide orange electrician's tape across the black tape, carefully trimming the excess tape with a crafts knife. Set the squash on the truck base.

Happy Owl-Oween!

Trace the patterns, *below*, onto tracing paper and cut out. Transfer the face and feathers pattern onto the pumpkin (see "Creative Carving Basics," page 46). Using a knife or carving tools, cut the eye and beak openings. Use a gouge to cut the chest feathers, going just deep enough to reveal the orange inner rind.

Fill the openings with pieces of crumpled newspaper. Spray-paint the pumpkin off-white; let dry. Regouge the chest feathers.

Cut outer ears from black cardstock and inner ears from patterned orange cardstock. Cut outer wings from patterned brown cardstock and inner wings from patterned orange cardstock. Glue the ear shapes together; glue the wing shapes together. Glue the wings to black cardstock; cut out, leaving a ⅛-inch black border all around. Fold and clip the ears and wings as noted on the patterns. Attach to the pumpkin with straight pins.

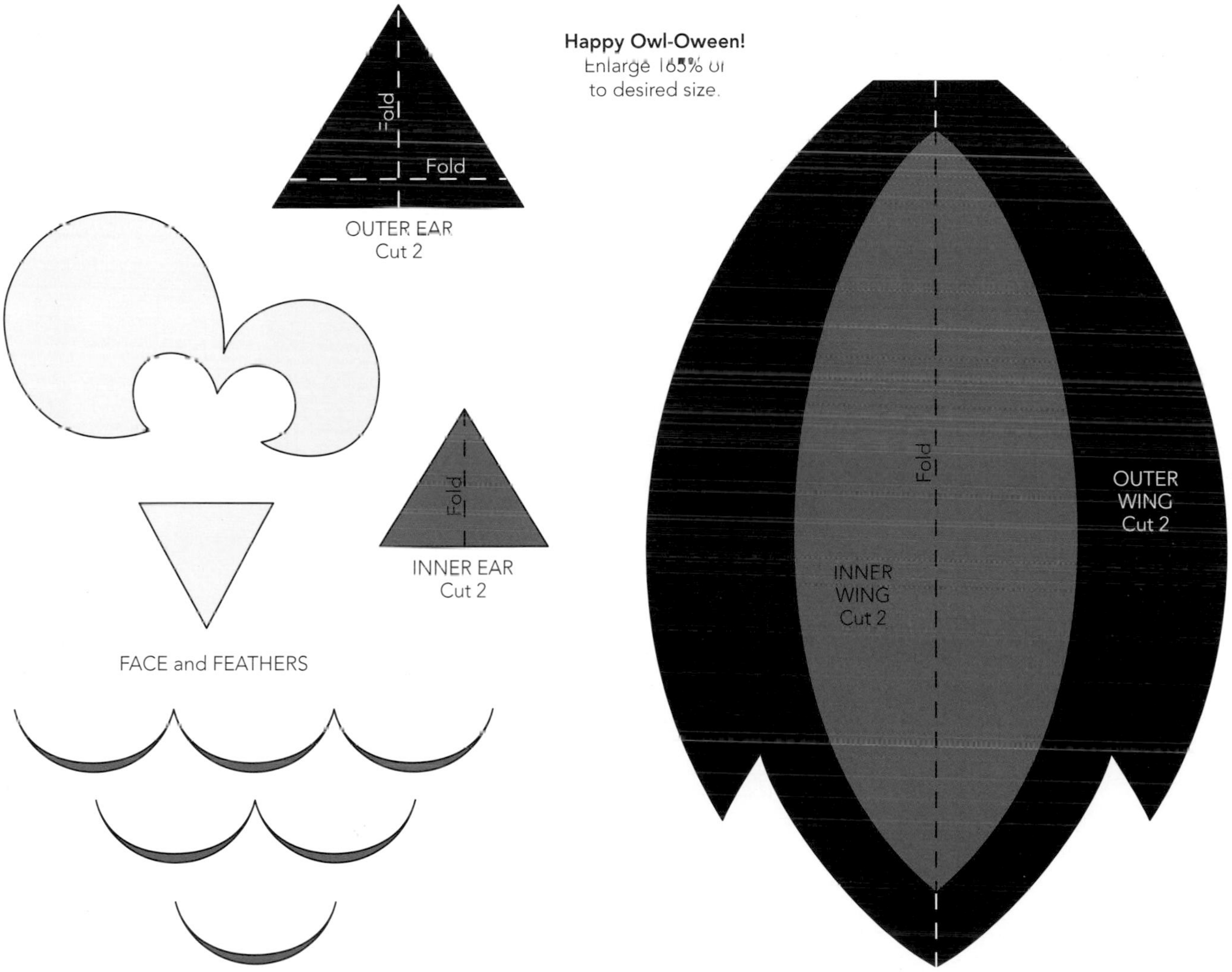

They're Having a Ball

Note: See "Creative Carving Basics," page 46, for a guide to tools, tips, and techniques such as transferring patterns.

Transfer the desired patterns, *opposite*, onto the pumpkins. Use paint or markers to add detail and color to the features.

With a gouge, cut circles for eyes. Insert purchased eyeball rubber balls (found at party supply stores), marbles, or other patterned balls into the gouged openings. Add zany pupils or extra details with colored markers.

Trompe l'Oeil Treat

Cover the stem of a cone-shape orange pumpkin with painter's tape. Spray-paint the bottom third of the pumpkin yellow and the top third white. Let dry after each color application.

Boo-rah!

Paint the pumpkin stem using black crafts paint; let dry. Copy and enlarge the letters, *below,* to fit the front of the pumpkin; cut out. Position the cutout letter patterns on the pumpkin, and trace around them with a pencil. Fill each letter outline with black buttons, adhering the buttons with glue. Tie black wire-edged ribbon into a bow around the pumpkin stem.

Web Crawlers

Completely cover the stems of pie pumpkins with painter's tape. Spray-paint the pumpkins black; let dry.

Brush crafts glue, then liberal amounts of black glitter onto the pumpkins; let dry. Remove painter's tape from stem. Attach

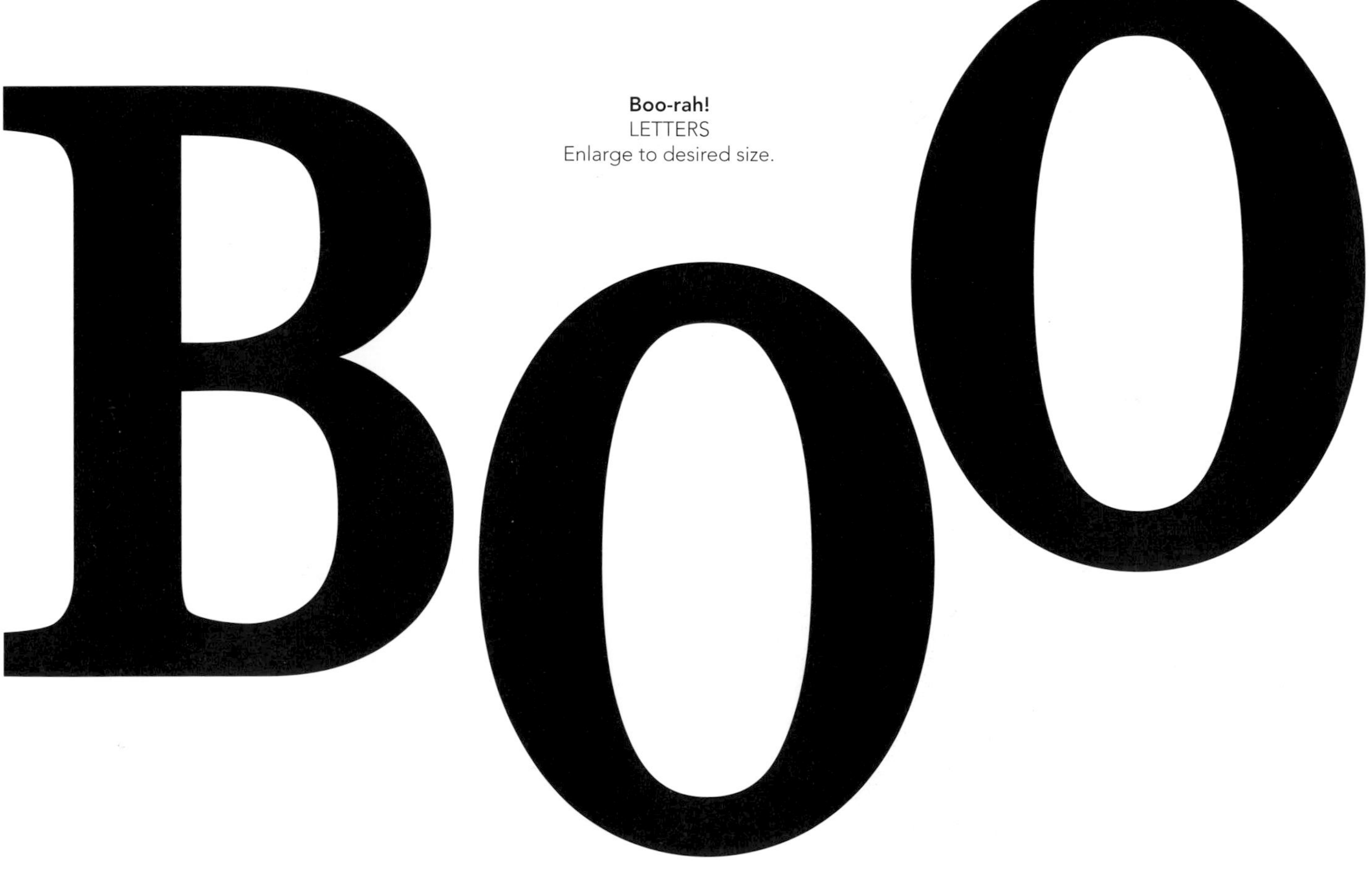

Boo-rah!
LETTERS
Enlarge to desired size.

eight black bumpy chenille stems for legs by poking the ends into each pumpkin. Glue a pair of googly eyes to the front of each pumpkin.

They're Having a Ball
FACES
Enlarge to desired size.

pumpkin PETS ON PARADE

Create a lineup of whimsical pumpkin critters with super-simple materials and easy assembly that will have you looking at seasonal produce in a whole new way.

PRODUCED BY **MATTHEW MEAD**
WRITTEN BY **DEBRA WITTRUP**
PHOTOGRAPHY BY **REED DAVIS**

here, kitty, kitty
Set a medium-size pumpkin atop a larger pumpkin and you have the beginning of a fabulous feline, *opposite*. Using our patterns, *page 26*, pin or glue paper ears and facial features to the top pumpkin. Push in wire whiskers to bristle on each side of the nose. Finish with a paper-chain tail and a couple of pumpkin squash paws.

pumpkin pooch
Create a playful pup that never needs feeding, walking, or training. A large elongated pumpkin on its side and a smaller pumpkin standing upright form the canine head and body, *left*. Place two squash next to the large pumpkin for back legs and two small pumpkin squash in front of the head for front paws. Using the patterns, *page 27*, cut and assemble the face and ear shapes; attach with glue. Add a paper-chain tail, and stand back to see if it wags.

jeepers creepers
Little Miss Muffet doesn't stand a chance! Using the patterns, *page 26*, cut paper ovals and circles in ascending sizes for a spider's eyes. Stack and glue the shapes, and pin the eyes to the pumpkin. Glue together a narrow black strip and two freaky white fangs for the mouth. Pin the mouth to the pumpkin. Insert four wires into the pumpkin on each side of the face and bend to create eight creepy-crawly legs for this wicked spider, *left*.

With adult help, even young children can create their own pumpkin animals.

sneaky snake

This snake, *above*, looks like one laid-back reptile. But is he just chilling or waiting for a killing? Cover a row of pie pumpkins with groovy shapes punched from paper. Pin or glue the shapes in random patterns to all but one pumpkin. Cut facial features using the patterns, *page 26*, and assemble using the photo as a guide. Pin or glue the features to the head pumpkin. Now be smart and stay out of striking distance.

what a hoot!

Forget wise—this owl looks downright grumpy! Make this serious sentinel, *right*, with a small round pumpkin atop a larger elongated one. Cut and fold the face shapes and wings according to the patterns, *page 26*. Glue the pieces together, and pin them to the pumpkins.

DESIGNED BY KRISTIN CLEVELAND & WADE SCHERRER PHOTOGRAPHY BY GREG SCHEIDEMANN

good boy
A little carving creates this special pumpkin puppy, *above*. Cut out the bottoms and clean out a medium pumpkin for the head and a large elongated pumpkin for the body. Save the bottoms. Trim the stem on the large pumpkin even with its top. Transfer the patterns, *page 27*, onto the pumpkins (see "Creative Carving Basics," *page 46*). Using a knife or carving tools, cut out the openings. With a gouge, carve the tongue, eyes, and chest, scraping just deep enough to reveal the rind. Secure the gourd tail, ears, and feet with skewers. Attach a half radish for the nose. Set a candle or battery-operated light on the bottom of the body pumpkin; secure the body to its bottom with skewers. In the same way, secure the bottom of the head pumpkin to the top of the body pumpkin. Add a candle or battery-operated light, and secure the head in place with skewers. Hot-glue sunflower seeds to the face for whiskers, and wrap the neck with a dog collar.

Here, Kitty, Kitty
Enlarge to desired size.

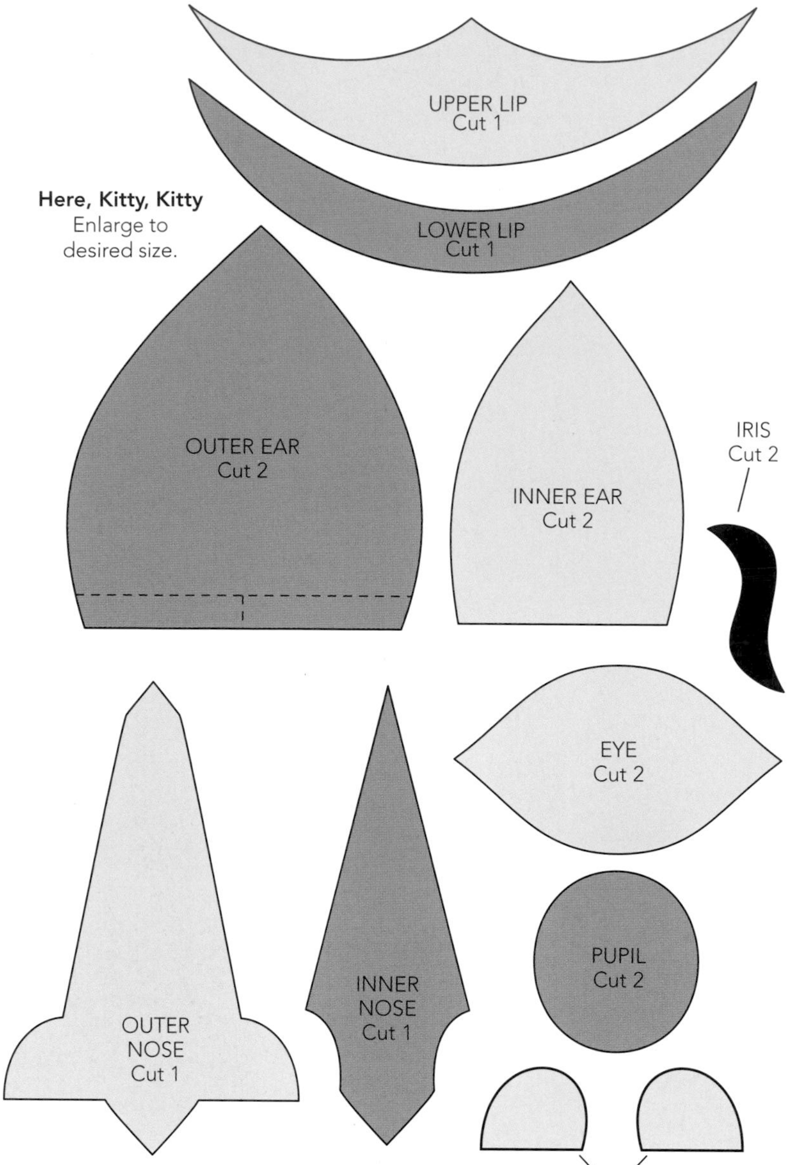

What a Hoot!
Enlarge to desired size.

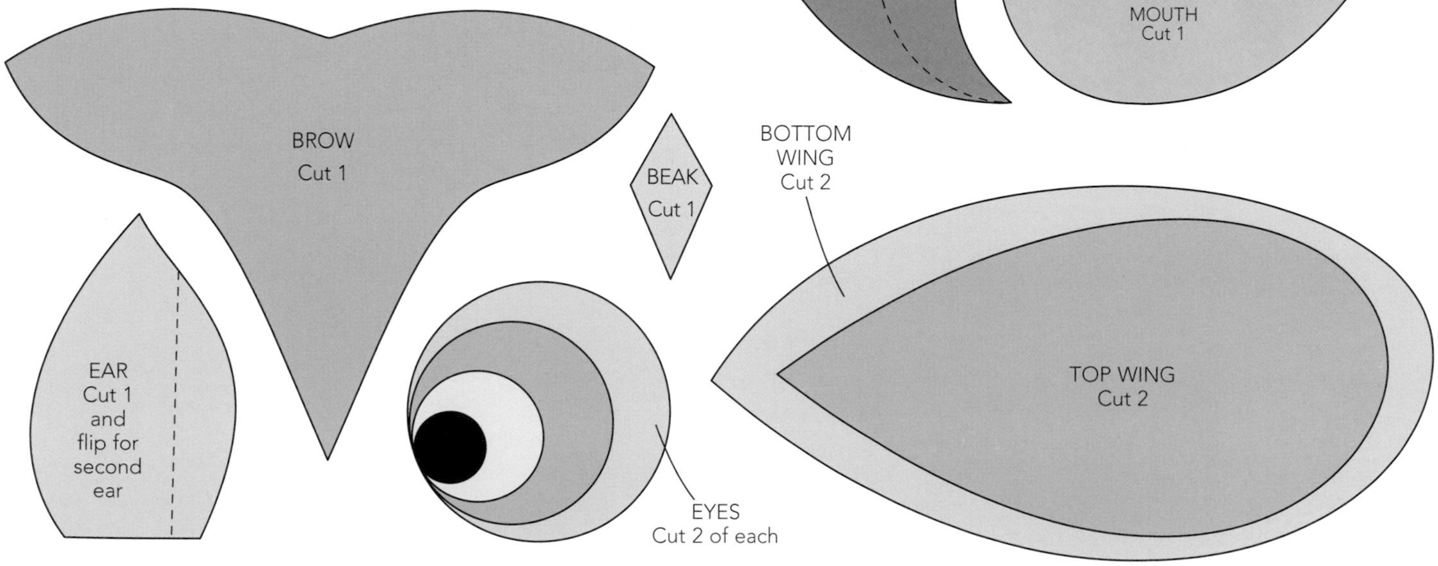

Jeepers Creepers
Enlarge to desired size.

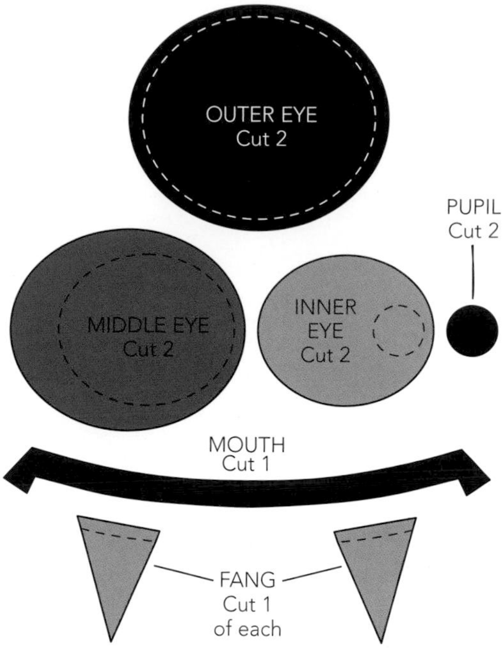

Sneaky Snake
Enlarge to desired size.

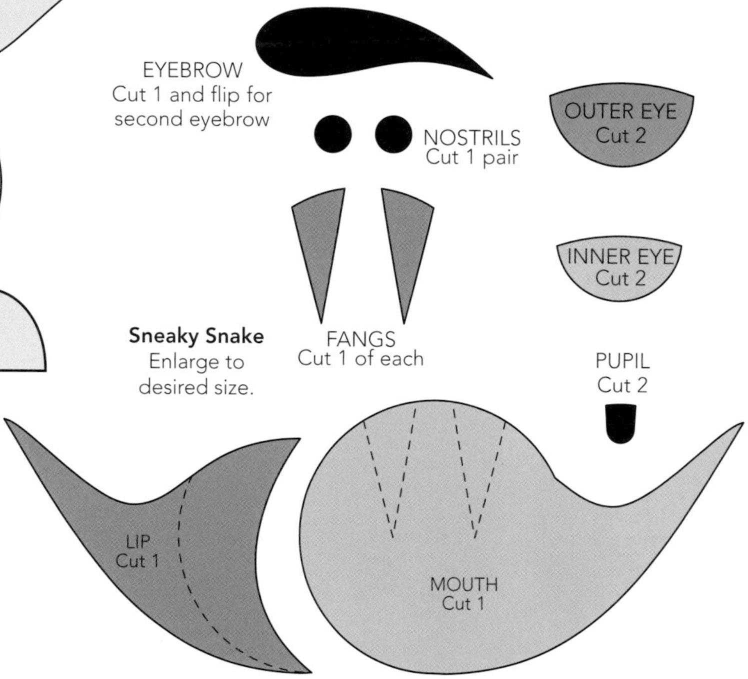

Pumpkin Pooch
Enlarge to desired size.

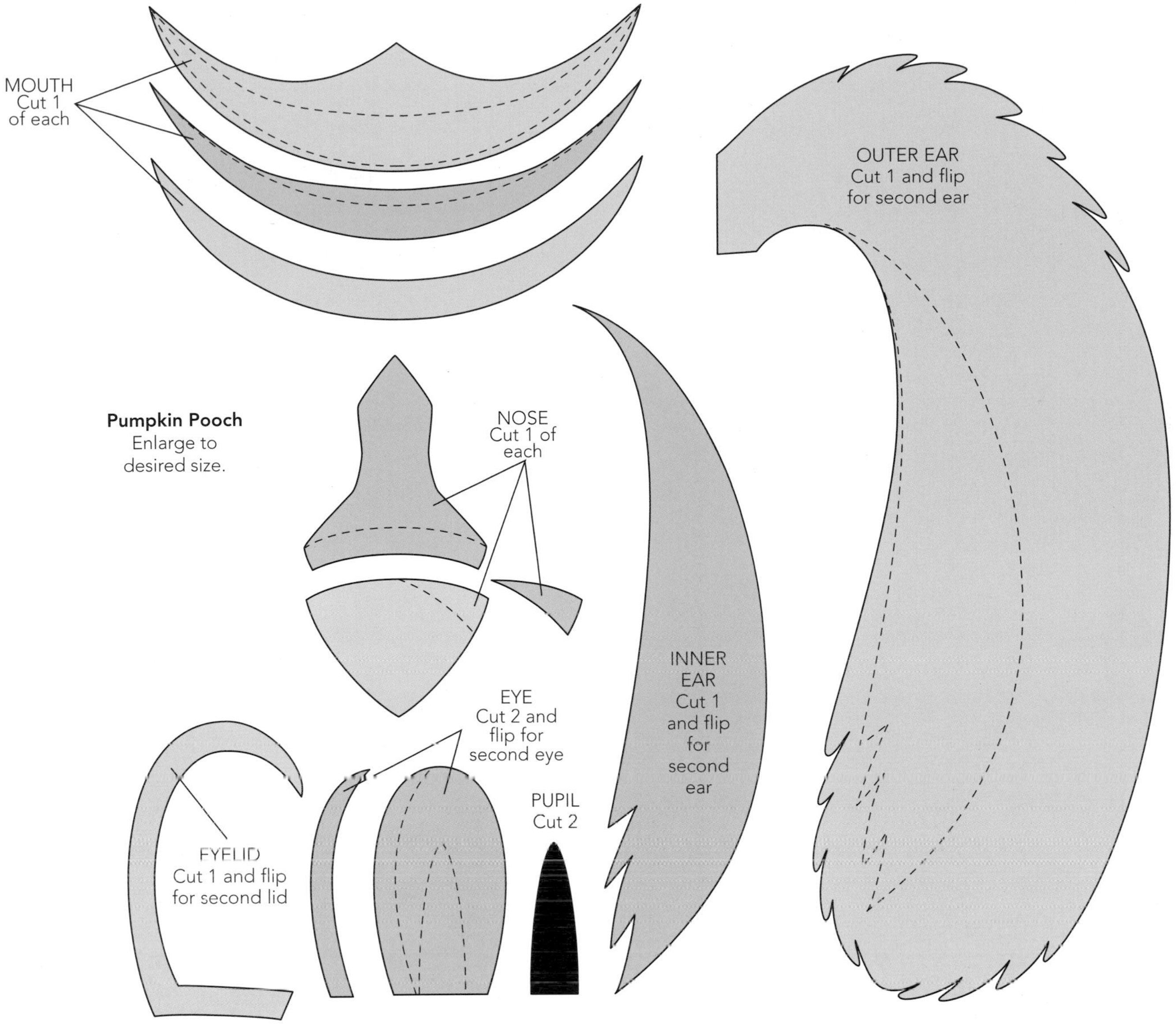

Good Boy
Enlarge to desired size.

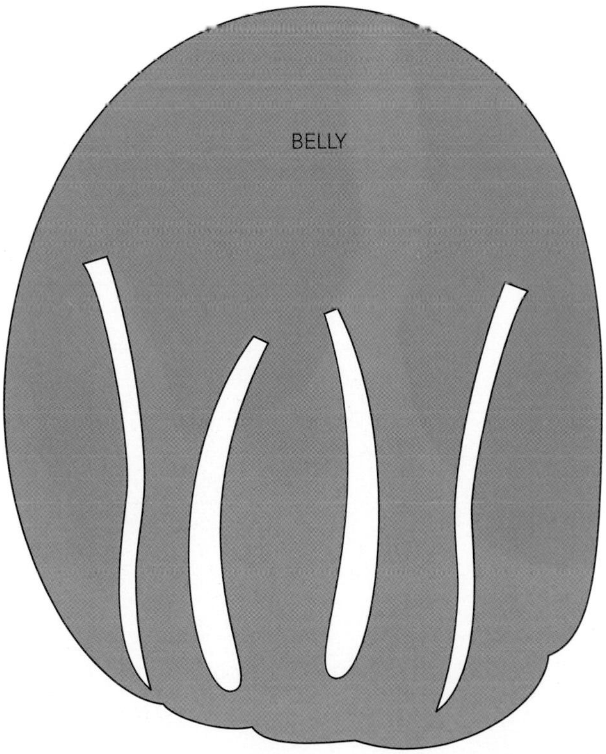

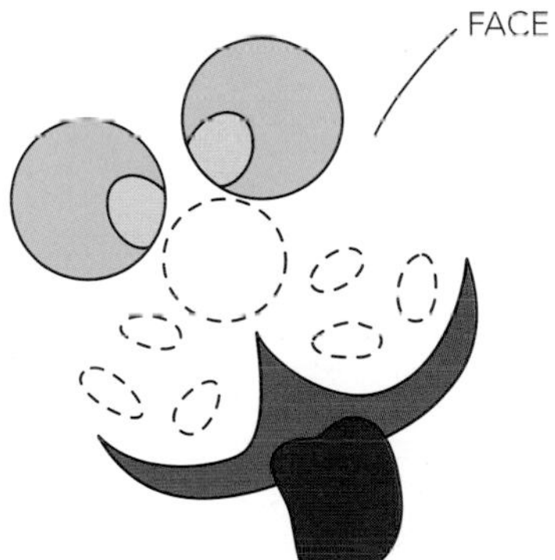

HALLOWEEN STARS

Ready to make merry (or scary) this Halloween? It's easy with clever carved designs and our instructions. Pick one or a handful to raise spirits all around the house.

take us to your leader
Greet trick-or-treaters at your door with these artful aliens. More goofy than ghoulish, each little E.T. has an eye or three crafted from clear ornament halves and crafts foam. See how they pop up in the most unusual places?

Use creepy-crawlies, bats, rats, and more to heighten the horror around your home.

eye-yi-yi—eyes!
Losing your marbles? It's understandable with all these eerie eyes, *above,* staring at you. Pairs of almond shapes, carved into a pumpkin, are just the right size to grip cat's-eye marbles.

this witch has rhythm
Tall pumpkins set the stage for the soft-shoe scenario, *above.* All you'll need to keep in step are the pumpkins, black paint, matching ribbon, our pattern, and shallow carving.

going batty in the belfry
Turn your pumpkin into architecture, such as this belfry, *opposite,* an attic, or even a single window. All you have to do to make it hair-raising is let loose a swarm of plastic bats.

Costume jewelry, kitchen accessories, thrift-store clothing, and garden tools can turn basic carved faces into striking personalities.

aunt hattie
No need for carving tools to conjure the spirit of lovable Aunt Hattie, *above left*. With a little dress-up fun, you can raise a whole wacky pumpkin family to welcome guests to your home.

cuisine art
Welcome candy-craving kids with this culinary critter, *above*. Our happy chef has a nose—a gourd, actually—for sniffing out the sweetest Halloween treats.

oopsie-daisy
This Halloween speed demon made a rough landing, *above*, but re-creating her is a breeze with witchy wardrobe items and stocking-striped sticks. Her hat, shoes, and cape can be found online or at theatrical shops.

home alone
With a toothy howl and eyeballs askew, this gourd, *above right*, looks as if he's seen a ghost. To let him raise his hands in horror, perch the carved face atop a pair of stuffed garden gloves.

halloween daze
To channel the spirits of Halloween, gaze into these hypnotic eyes, *above*. Any mouth and nose shape will work, as long as you carve mesmerizing eye spirals to create their zombielike trances.

mouse house
The plastic mice caught in the act of squeezing into this cheesy condo, *above right*, will make your trick-or-treaters shriek with fright.

letter-perfect
If your style is more sophisticated than silly, a monogram may be just the thing to personalize your pumpkins, *opposite*. To imitate our design, use your computer to choose a font and print the desired monogram. Enlarge the letter, cut it out, and use it as a pattern for cutting or gouging out the design.

h
H
H

When Halloween approaches, replace summer's fading flowers with pumpkin personalities tucked into empty urns and other garden containers.

the royal court
This royal couple, *opposite,* is more Alice in Wonderland than William and Kate, so the free-form facial features are left a little to the imagination. With carved pumpkin crowns atop their Expressionist heads, they're bound to be the rulers of your castle.

pumpkins with a voice
Who says pumpkins have to wear faces for Halloween? These orange gourds, *above,* clearly have something to say, and they do it with serious fall flair.

candy
this
HAPPY HALLOWEEN

no tricks, just treats

Let's not sugarcoat it—trick-or-treaters are in it for the candy. Show them the way with this satisfying trio of pumpkins dressed up as wrapped candies, *opposite*. All you need is a steady hand to chisel a message in the surfaces of the pumpkins and decorated dowels to mount your plastic-wrapped creations. But be warned, with signage like this, you'll need plenty of treats on hand!

rough and tough

Are this guy's bumps and bruises the result of pumpkin roughhousing? No, they're just an ingenious way to take advantage of not-so-perfect pumpkins. Choose an unripe or dirty pumpkin, then add cockscomb contusions, bulging gourd eyes, and crooked candy-corn teeth for a head-reeling effect, *above left*.

use your head

No bones about it, this smiling skull, *above*, has personality. He gets his spirited attitude from a spray-painted gourd detailed with painted facial features, metal washer eyes, and a mini top hat. A seasonal candle stand serves as his skeletal frame.

CARVING TIPS
Before starting your pumpkin project, check out our tested "Creative Carving Basics," page 46, for a guide to tools, tips, and techniques such as transferring patterns.

Take Us to Your Leader

If desired, use a gray pumpkin for an alien carving (the inside of this type of pumpkin is naturally a vibrant orange). Transfer the face patterns, *below,* onto the pumpkins.

Using a knife or carving tools, cut out the openings. Use a gouge to cut into the teeth, cutting just deep enough to make them "pearly whites." Drill holes into the pumpkins large enough to hold the gourd antennae (on the left and center pumpkins) and the gourd nose (on the right pumpkin).

For eyeballs, paint the outside of clear plastic ornament halves (the kind that you open and fill) in bright colors; let dry. Cut large white circles and smaller black circles from crafts foam for eyes. Glue the circles together and add red veins using a felt-tip marking pen. Hot-glue the eyes onto the inside of the painted eyeballs. Except for the one-eyed alien, hot-glue the assembled eyes in place. For the one-eyed alien, cut a circular hole in the front of the pumpkin and slip an eyeball in place. If desired, cut a tongue from pink crafts foam and slip it into an alien mouth.

Eye-Yi-Yi—Eyes!

Transfer the pattern pair, *below,* multiple times to the front of a pumpkin. Using a knife or carving tools, cut out the openings. Place cotton balls in the eye openings, and spray-paint the pumpkin black. Let the paint dry and remove the cotton balls. Slip a marble into each eye.

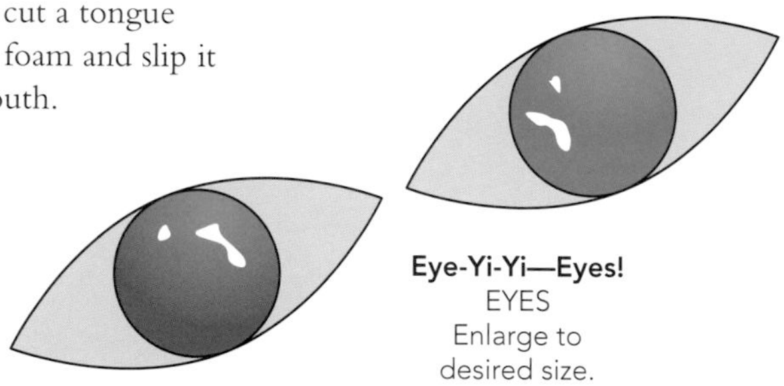

Eye-Yi-Yi—Eyes!
EYES
Enlarge to desired size.

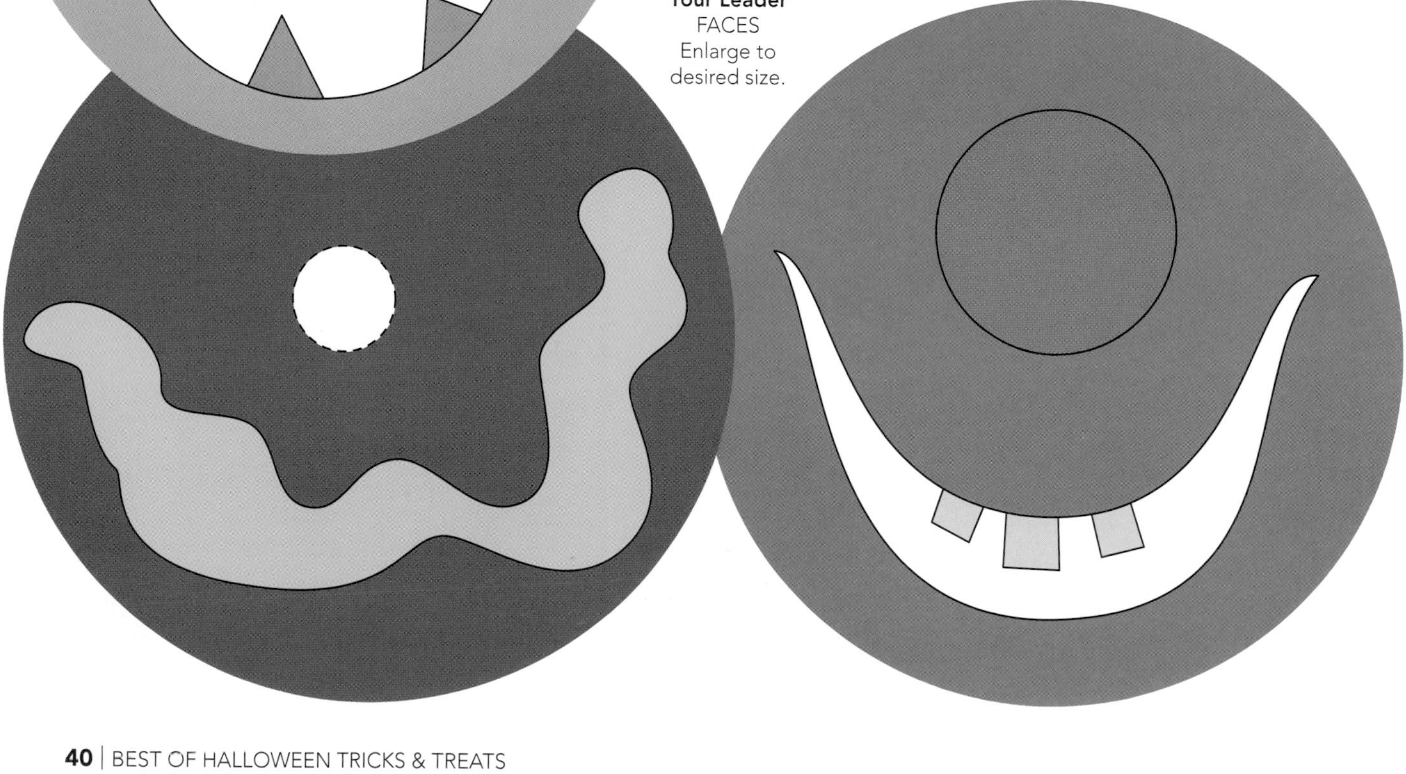

Take Us to Your Leader
FACES
Enlarge to desired size.

This Witch Has Rhythm

Transfer the patterns, *below right,* onto two tall pumpkins. Using a gouge, carve narrow, alternating stocking stripes. Paint the shoes and uncarved stocking stripes black. Tie two bows using grosgrain ribbon, and pin the bows to the shoes with straight pins or T-pins.

Going Batty in the Belfry

Transfer the pattern, *below left,* onto the pumpkin. Using a knife or carving tools, cut out the openings. With a gouge, cut the shingles, going just deep enough to reveal the pumpkin's inner rind. Paint the roof and belfry outlines black.

Cut three lengths of heavy-gauge wire. Push one end of each wire into a plastic bat, and push the wired bats into the pumpkin.

Aunt Hattie

Choose a pumpkin with a stem that will work for a nose. Carve a small slit below the stem to insert wax lips. Use post earrings for eyes, and push them into the pumpkin. Set (folded) eyeglasses in place and mark a dot at each temple. At each dot, cut a slit large enough to slip the eyeglass bows into the pumpkin. Use long pins to secure chandelier crystals (or crystal beads from crafts stores) for earrings. Top the pumpkin with a lampshade that fits the shape, decorating the shade with costume jewelry pins and beaded trim hot-glued around the edge.

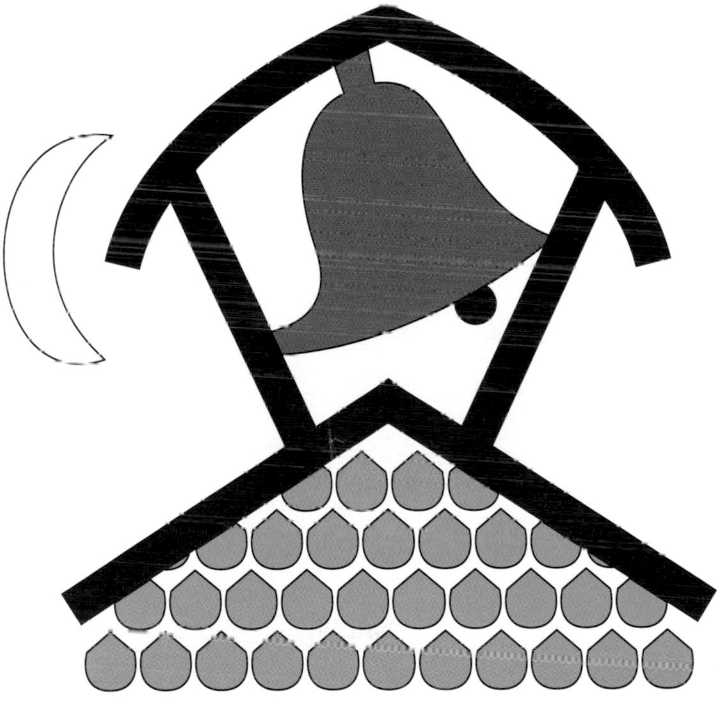

Going Batty in the Belfry
ROOFTOP & BELL
Enlarge to desired size.

This Witch Has Rhythm
LEGS
Enlarge to desired size.

Cuisine Art

Use a gray pumpkin for the rat chef. Cut a circle from the bottom of the pumpkin.

Cut two ears from the pumpkin circle. Transfer the eyes and mouth patterns, *below,* onto the pumpkin. Using a knife or carving tools, cut out the eye openings. Use a gouge to carve a thin mouth, carving just deep enough to reveal the inner rind. Use half of a gourd for the nose and attach it using wood skewers. Push pieces of floral cloth-covered wire into the nose for whiskers. Insert ears into cutout slots in each side of the pumpkin. Add a chef's hat, a wire whisk, and a checkered dish towel to complete the design.

Oopsie-Daisy!

Transfer the pattern, *below right,* onto the pumpkin, placing the pattern so the stem works for the nose. Using a knife or carving tools, cut out the openings. Use a gouge to cut into the eye pupils and to cut the lines around the eyes, cutting just deep enough to reveal the pumpkin's inner rind.

Choose two long, sturdy tree branches from your yard for legs. Wrap each with white and red duct tape, alternating the colors and creating evenly spaced stripes. Place the witch hat on the ground, and on top of it, put the pumpkin face upside-down. Push the legs into the ground behind the pumpkin and add shoes. Drape a cape or black fabric on the ground around the pumpkin.

Home Alone

Transfer the pattern, *opposite right,* onto the pumpkin. Using a knife or carving tools, cut out the openings. With a gouge, cut into the teeth, cutting just deep enough to reveal the inner rind.

Lightly stuff garden gloves with fiberfill. Slip a length of thin-gauge wire, bent into a circle at one end, into each finger and thumb. Tuck the gloves under the pumpkin face and shape them to create the desired effect.

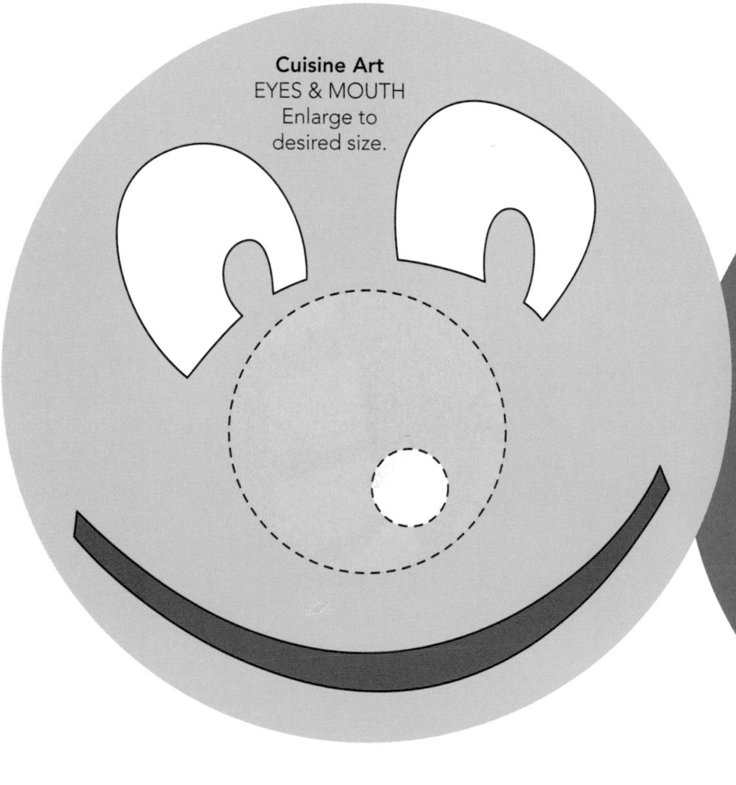

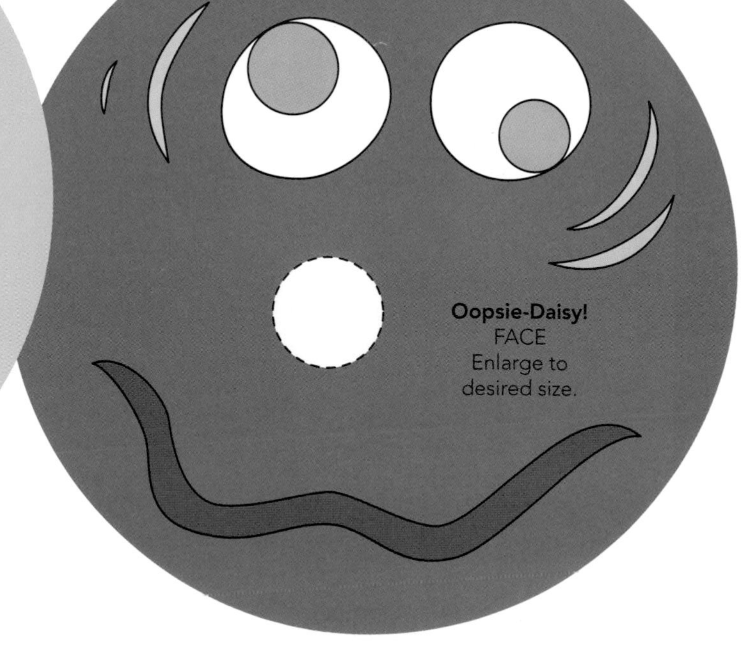

Halloween Daze

Transfer a face pattern, *below,* onto a white pumpkin. Using a knife or carving tools, cut out the openings for the features.

Mouse House

Use a drill and ½- and 1-inch flat wood bits to drill holes in the pumpkin. Carefully covering the cut edges of the holes, spray-paint the pumpkin surface light yellow. Add plastic mice.

Letter-Perfect

Select a font from your computer. Enlarge the monogram letter to fit your pumpkin and print it out. Transfer the letter pattern to the pumpkin. Using a knife or carving tools, cut out the openings or gouge just deep enough to reveal the inner rind.

Halloween Daze
FACES
Enlarge to desired size.

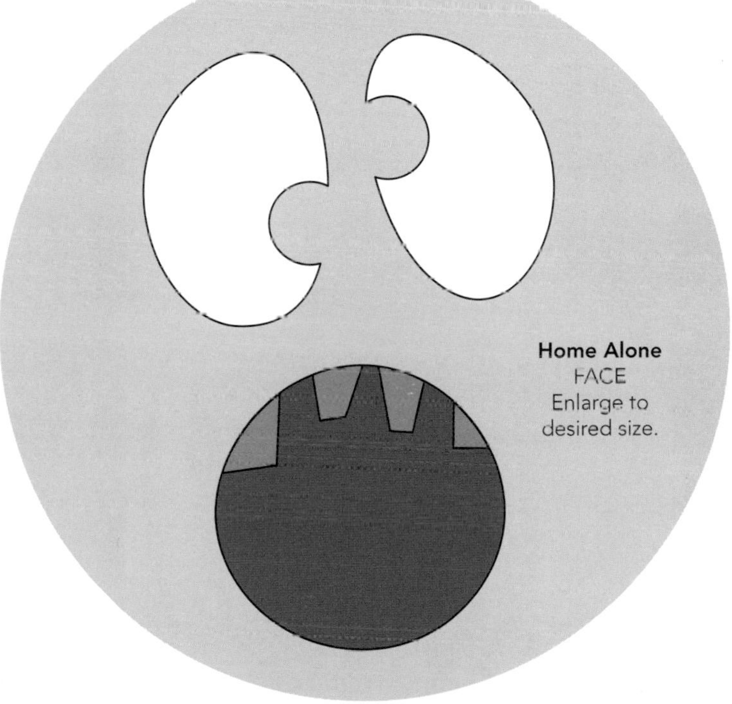

Home Alone
FACE
Enlarge to desired size.

The Royal Court

Transfer the face patterns, *bottom,* onto the pumpkins. Using a knife or carving tools, cut out the openings. With a gouge, cut the facial lines, going just deep enough to reveal the inner rinds.

Cut the crowns from the top and bottom of a third pumpkin. Using a gouge and the patterns, *below right,* cut the outlines for the jewels. Attach purchased faux gems to the gouged areas on both crowns with crafts glue. Thread more pearls onto pearl-head pins and attach them to the scalloped edge of one of the crowns.

Use skewers to attach the crowns to the tops of the pumpkins. Add strips of faux fur and lace as collars around the bases of the pumpkins.

Pumpkins with a Voice

Using assorted fonts on your computer, create the message. Enlarge the words to fit the pumpkins and print them out. Transfer the words to the pumpkins, placing them in a straight line, a curve, or jumping up and down to make the most appealing pattern. Using a knife or carving tools, cut out the words.

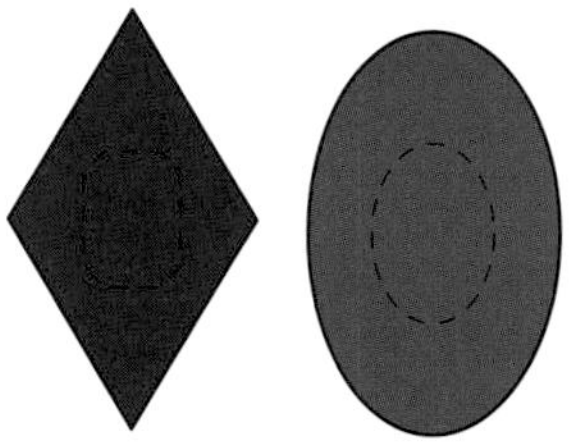

The Royal Court
JEWEL OUTLINES
Enlarge to desired size.

No Tricks, Just Treats

Transfer each sign pattern, *opposite left,* onto a pumpkin. With a gouge, cut around the letters, going just deep enough to reveal the pumpkins' inner rinds. Outline the letters with black marker, and decorate with stripes and polka dots as you like.

Remove the stems from the pumpkins. Wrap a sheet of cellophane around each pumpkin, tying the excess at the sides with ribbon. Cut a small slit in the cellophane above the stem base. Hot-glue the stem back onto the top of the pumpkin through the slit.

Cut three 1- to 2-inch-diameter dowels to the desired length for mounting posts. Using a crafts knife, whittle one end of each dowel to a point. Cover the posts with black scrapbooking paper and embellish with Halloween-theme ribbon.

The Royal Court
FACES
Enlarge to desired size.

Push the dowels into the ground with the pointed ends up. Spear the pumpkins onto the pointed dowels.

Rough and Tough

Transfer the patterns, *below right,* onto a dirty or unripe pumpkin. Using a knife or carving tools, cut out the openings.

Use a knife to slice the bottoms off two gourds. Attach the gourd bottoms to the eye openings using wooden skewers. Cut a piece of cockscomb, and insert it into the head opening above the right eye using wooden skewers. Hot-glue candy corn to pieces of heavy paper that fit the mouth opening, and glue to the mouth.

Use Your Head

Spray-paint a butternut squash white. Transfer the patterns, *bottom right,* onto the painted squash. Using a small paintbrush, paint the cranial fissures, the nose, and the smile with black crafts paint. Cut ovals from black felt for the

eyes and hot-glue to the squash as shown, *above*. Hot-glue 1-inch-diameter metal washers to the felt ovals for the pupils. Glue a purchased miniature top hat to the top of the squash. Display on an appropriate stand or as desired.

Rough and Tough
FACE
Enlarge to desired size.

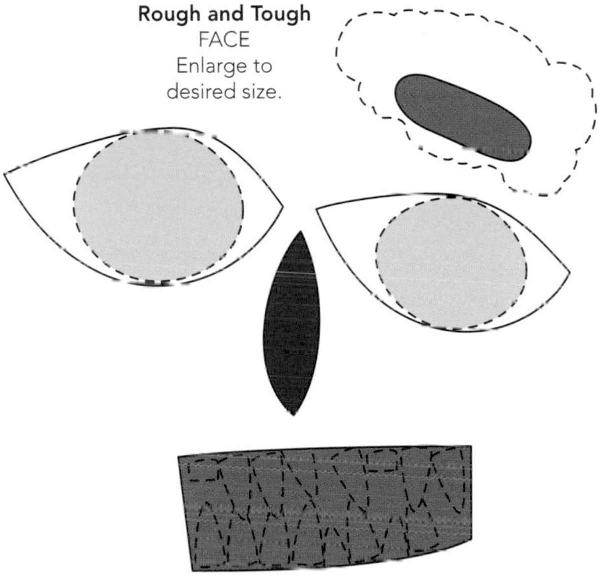

No Tricks, Just Treats
SIGN DESIGNS
Enlarge to desired size.

Use Your Head
FACE
Enlarge to desired size.

creative CARVING BASICS

Follow our tips and techniques to make your next jack-o'-lanterns the stars of your neighborhood.

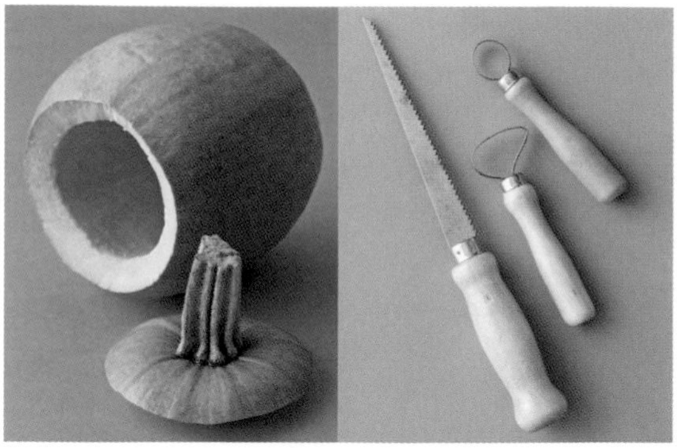

Prepare the Pumpkin

Draw the lid outline on top of a room-temperature pumpkin, or draw a circle on the pumpkin bottom. Make a notch at the back to use as a guide for replacing the lid or bottom. Cut along the lines using a keyhole saw. The long blade is best for cutting through the thick pumpkin rind. Clean out the seeds and pulp using a large spoon. Scrape the inside of the pumpkin with clay-modeling tools until the walls are about 1 inch thick.

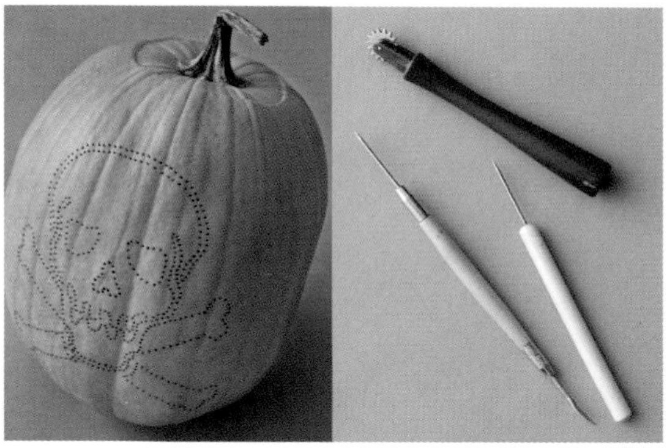

Transfer the Design

Choose a carving pattern. Enlarge or reduce the pattern to fit your pumpkin. Tape or pin the pattern to the pumpkin; transfer the pattern using graphite paper and a tracing wheel (found at fabrics stores), or poke the holes using an awl or ceramics tool. If using a poker-type tool, push the point into the pumpkin skin but not through the pumpkin wall; space the holes about ⅛ inch apart.

Cut Shapes

Cradle the pumpkin in your lap and use a crafts knife to cut out the designs. For smaller openings, use a fine-tooth saw. Grasp the saw as you would hold a pencil and cut with a continuous up-and-down motion, keeping the saw perpendicular to the pumpkin. Apply gentle pressure and work from the center out on large designs. Remove and reinsert the knife to make corners; avoid twisting the blade as you work.

Coat the cut edges of your pumpkin with petroleum jelly to help it last longer.

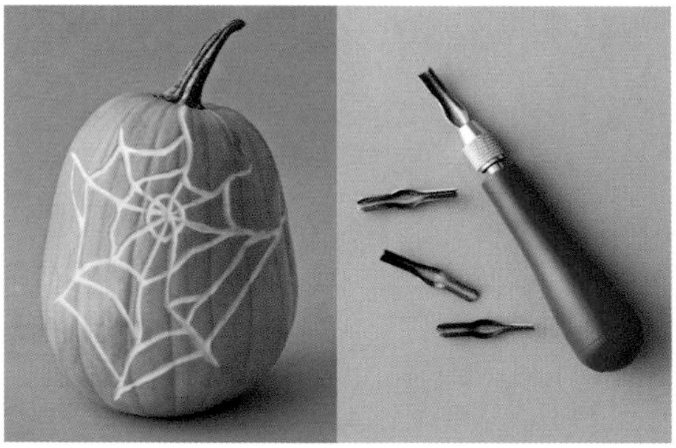

Gouge Design Lines

Wood-carving gouges work well to remove strips of skin from a pumpkin. Gouged areas glow when light shines through from the inside. Experiment with different gouge sizes to vary the line width. Along pattern lines, carefully remove skin and some pulp until the pumpkin wall is the desired thickness.

Gouge Out Large Areas

In addition to gouging fine lines, wood-carving gouges can be utilized for removing large areas of pumpkin skin. Choose the widest rounded gouge for the largest areas to be gouged, and use narrower gouges for more intricate designs. The deeper the gouge in the pumpkin wall, the more the light will shine through.

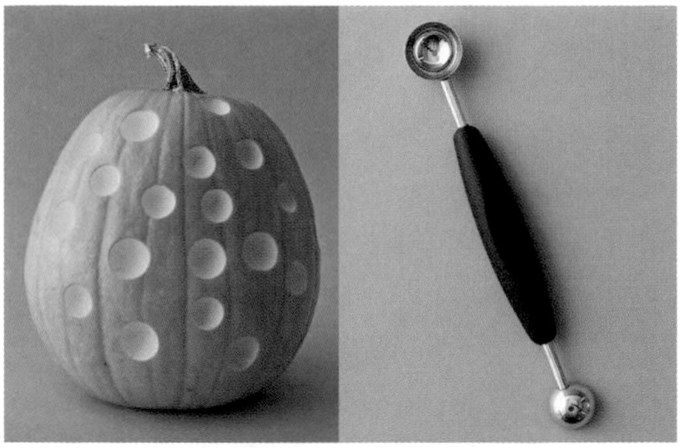

Scoop Out Circular Shapes

To create glowing round shapes, use a melon baller to scoop out circular areas of the pumpkin skin. Push one edge of the melon baller into the pumpkin to break the skin, and gently push the baller to scoop out the area. Repeat this process to create depressions all over the pumpkin. Place a light inside the pumpkin to make the scooped-out areas glow.

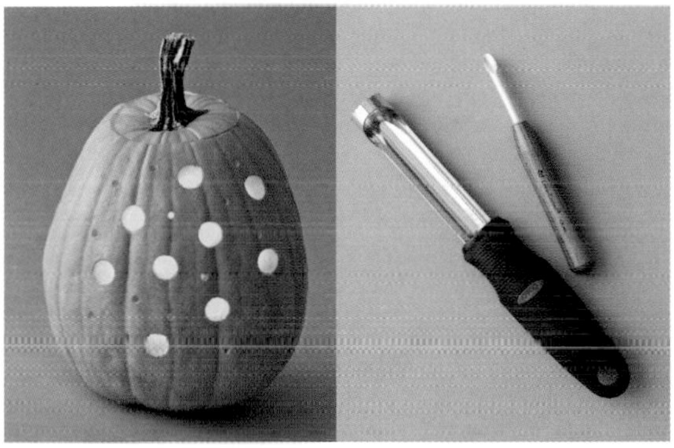

Cut Perfect Holes

If you want large holes in your pumpkin, it isn't always practical to use a fine-tooth saw to cut out the shape. To get a perfect circle every time, an apple corer is easy and efficient to use. Push the sharp round end of the corer through the pumpkin wall. A pottery tool also can be used to pierce a pumpkin with smaller holes.

Avoid any potential fire hazard by lighting your jack-o'-lantern with a battery-powered light rather than a candle.

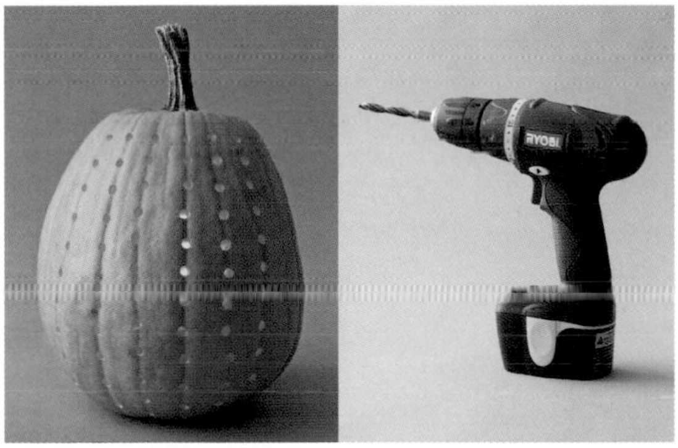

Drill Holes

For the fastest and easiest way to make holes in a pumpkin, use a power drill. Experiment with drill bit sizes and patterns for different effects. For example, follow the ribs on a pumpkin or create allover patterns. If desired, insert string lights in the drilled holes.

Cut Shapes with Cookie Cutters

Metal cookie cutters are good for cutting out fancy shapes without having to use a saw. Place the sharp edge of a cutter against the pumpkin, then use a hammer or rubber mallet to tap the cutter into the pumpkin skin. Continue tapping the cutter until it breaks through the pumpkin wall.

Something's brewing...

parties

There's no disguising how much fun you can have at a Halloween party. Get just a little freaky with your grown-up friends or scare up wholesome kid-friendly amusement. Invitations, menus, activities, decorations—everything you need to host a memorable gathering is at your fingertips.

WELCOME ALL SPIRITS

Host a haunting night of "groan-up" thrills and chills, where ghostly figures haunt the halls and dead men do tell tales.

PRODUCED AND WRITTEN BY **DEBRA WITTRUP**
PAPER PROJECTS BY **BRANDY FAULKNER**
FOOD STYLED BY **JENNIFER PETERSON**
PHOTOGRAPHY BY **GREG SCHEIDEMANN**

Project instructions and recipes begin on *page 58*.

melancholy mansion
Stage a somber scene at the front door with twin pumpkin towers, *opposite*. Lace-wrapped pumpkins ascend from lightweight urns that feature a spray-painted stone look. Pleats of lace line the top of each urn, and a black bow decorates the base.

ominous invitation
Summon the supernatural with a party invitation, *above*, crafted from distressed and ink-stained cardstock. The agitated apparition on the front foreshadows a hair-raising celebration.

Withered
Zombie
Vengeful
Vodka

Abandon hope, all ye who enter.

Cross the threshold into another dimension where elegance and a spine-tingling atmosphere set the stage for a night of good food, friends, and fun.

For our ill-omened wake, we set the scene with tarnished family silver, yards of black and gray lace, and moody photographs. Spectral visitors emerge from behind flea market finds marked with the patina of time. If your day-to-day furnishings are too cheerful for such a frightful scene, drape them with tea-stained sheets and hang tattered cheesecloth at the windows. Use flickering candlelight to create lots of shadowy dark corners.

Liven up your celebration with a food and refreshment presentation that suggests a mausoleum or crypt. Add to the funereal ambience with a crystal ball for predicting the future. Then be prepared: If you set a spirited scene, you may find a few spirits will visit.

spirits of the dearly departed

Invite guests to imbibe if they dare. Fashion frightful labels, *opposite,* for potent potables using our patterns on distressed paper. Give cocktail napkins a weathered finish, and line a frame, sprayed with ivory crackle paint, with lace to fashion a tray for "shock-tail" hour.

ghostly greeting

Compose an entry table, *above left,* that sets the tone for the evening ahead. Futures are forecast with a large crystal ball, while the morbid buffet offerings are heralded on a suitably weathered menu card.

macabre menu

Get extra mileage out of the menu card by using it as a guessing game, *above.* Challenge guests to match each creepy culinary creation with the real names of the food. Bleached Bones, anyone?

What could be more appropriate at a Halloween "wake" than serving your feast in a coffin? Offer plenty of food, then party until you wake the dead!

wake me when it's over
Raise the coffin to serving height with a table created from lightweight garden urns on plywood pedestals, *left*. Top the urns with a thick sheet of wood or a hollow-core door. Give the whole ensemble a stone-cold look with spray paint that mimics gray granite.

grave message
Use nailhead trim to put your sentiments on the clever coffin-inspired buffet table, *above*. But do the cryptic letters stand for Rest In Peace or Repast In Progress?

digestible digits

Finger foods, *above*, take on new meaning with a platter of Bitty Toes—breadsticks with sliced almond "nails"—and white asparagus "fingers" standing upright in a small urn. Both make excellent sauce dippers. Sausages in barbecue sauce are always a crowd pleaser—and will be a conversation starter when renamed Icky Intestines.

remains of the day

Served in a coffin on antique china and tarnished silver, this sinister smorgasbord, *right*, is full of appetizing anatomically named edibles. Our menu of tasty dishes alludes to body parts with appropriately gruesome names. Hand the printed bills of fare to your guests and watch them approach with trepidation and fascination.

soul food

The brains of the operation, *above right*, made of molded (not moldy) shrimp, are displayed on an elevated silver tray, while a standing rib roast looms invitingly.

haunting backdrop
Set the stage, *top*, for your ghoulish get-together with bookcases filled with ethereal ephemera. Clocks tick relentlessly toward the haunting hours, and spirited photos fill the frames.

dead head
A phantom presence, *above left*, emerges from the underworld and into the back of the bookcase. It's actually a papier-mâché mask and faux hand attached to a removable plywood panel.

lights in the night
Cast an eerie (and safe) glow, *above*, with battery-operated candles. Wrap the candles with aged book pages or newsprint, and group them on a silver tray for an otherworldly glimmer.

Go to **BHG.com/HTTbookSpirits** to download printable designs and patterns for these party projects.

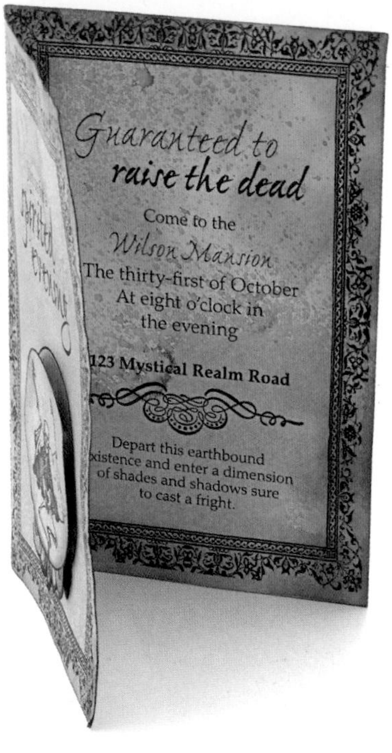

Ominous Invitation

MATERIALS

Cream cardstock
Walnut ink
Toothbrush
Fine-grit sandpaper
Distress ink in Brushed Corduroy
Ink blending tool (We used Inkssentials.)
Invitation patterns, *opposite*
Skeleton stamp
Black ink
Adhesive-foam dots

INSTRUCTIONS

Hang the cardstock on a line and spray lightly with walnut ink. (Protect the area around the cardstock from overspray.) Let dry. Dip a toothbrush into the ink and fleck more spots randomly; let dry.

Using sandpaper, rub along the cardstock edges to give it a worn look. Lightly ink the blending tool with Distress ink. Using circular motions, blend the ink onto the cardstock.

Photocopy the frame and text for the invitation cover and inside, *opposite*. Write or print the party details on the inside of the invitation. Test the layout by copying the patterns onto both sides of plain paper. When you are satisfied with the placement, copy the invitation designs onto the cardstock. Fold invitation.

Photocopy the crystal ball design, *opposite bottom*, separately onto distressed cardstock and cut it out. Ink the skeleton stamp with black ink and press onto the crystal ball design. Add Distress ink around the edges of the ball using the blending tool. Attach adhesive-foam dots to the back of the cutout and adhere to the front of the invitation.

Spirits of the Dearly Departed Napkins

MATERIALS

Cocktail napkins
Skeleton stamp
Scroll design stamp
Black ink pad (We used StazOn.)
Walnut ink

INSTRUCTIONS

Cover the work surface with newspapers. Insert a cardboard scrap into a napkin fold. Stamp the skeleton image and the scroll design onto the napkin using black ink. Lightly spray walnut ink on the napkin front. Let dry. Repeat for remaining napkins.

Spirits of the Dearly Departed Labels

INSTRUCTIONS

Distress cardstock following the invitation instructions, *left*.

Photocopy the label designs, *below*, onto distressed cardstock. Ink a scroll design stamp with black ink and press onto labels below the words. Add Distress ink around the edges of the labels using the blending tool.

Outline the circle with black marker, if desired. Cut out labels. Adhere the labels to the bottles using a glue stick.

Spirits of the Dearly Departed
LABEL DESIGNS

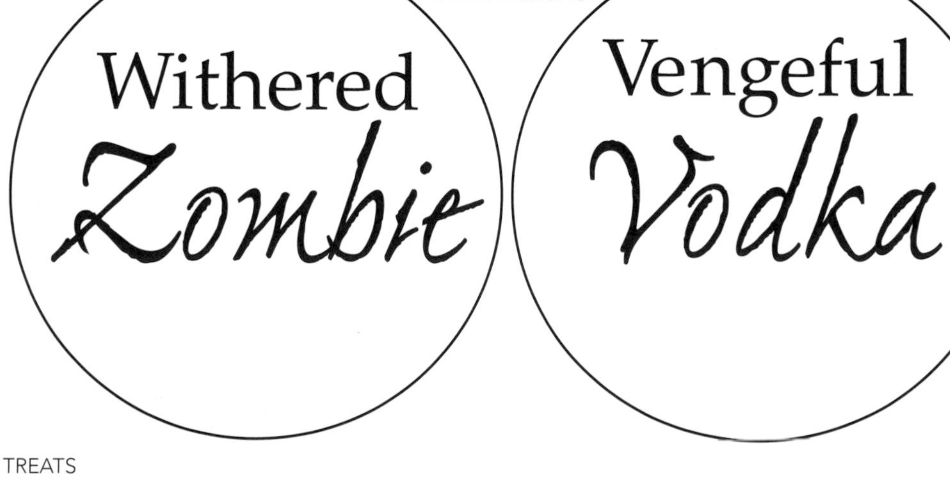

Guaranteed to
raise the dead

Depart this earthbound
existence and enter a dimension
of shades and shadows sure
to cast a fright.

Ominous Invitation COVER and INSIDE FRAMES AND TEXT

Join us for a
spirited
evening

Macabre Menu
CARD

Macabre Menu Card

INSTRUCTIONS

Distress cardstock following the invitation instructions, *page 58,* and photocopy the menu card, *below*, onto the cardstock. For display, adhere the menu to a black cardstock backing for stability.

Make additional menus to use as game cards. Have guests match the creepy offerings on the menu, *left*, with the real names below. (Provide the answers on a separate sheet.)

1. French Bread Heels
2. Herbed Breadsticks
3. Kidney Bean Salad
4. Macaroni Salad
5. White Asparagus Spears
6. Marinated Mozzarella
7. Shrimp Aspic
8. Raspberry Brie
9. Barbecue Sausages
10. Standing Rib Roast
11. French Dip Sandwiches
12. Glazed Sweet Breads
13. Chocolate Candies
14. Jelly Bean Candies
15. Tiramisu

Welcome To The
"Out of Body"
Experience!

Check each box as you find the anatomical parts that make up this evening's dining delights.

- ☐ Crusty Heels
- ☐ Bitty Toes
- ☐ Floating Kidneys
- ☐ Sharp Elbows
- ☐ Skeletal Fingers
- ☐ Staring Eyeballs
- ☐ Strained Brain
- ☐ Bleeding Brie Heart
- ☐ Icky Intestines
- ☐ Rattling Rib Cage
- ☐ Roasted Rump
- ☐ Bleached Bones
- ☐ Gallstones
- ☐ Belly Bits
- ☐ Graveyard Lady Fingers

Bitty Toes

One bite of these Herbed Breadsticks, and you'll be back for another… and another… and another.

PREP: 25 minutes
BAKE: 10 minutes

INGREDIENTS

- 1 11-ounce package (12) refrigerated breadsticks
- 36 almond slices (about 1 tablespoon)
- 2 tablespoons butter, melted
- ½ teaspoon dried Italian seasoning, crushed
- 2 tablespoons finely shredded Parmesan cheese

INSTRUCTIONS

Preheat oven to 375°F. Grease two baking sheets or line with parchment paper; set aside.

Separate breadstick dough at perforations to create 12 pieces. Cut each piece crosswise into three pieces. Arrange pieces on the prepared baking sheets. Taper one short end of each piece; press an almond into the tapered end to resemble a toenail.

In a small bowl stir together butter and Italian seasoning. Brush over dough. Sprinkle each with Parmesan cheese.

Bake for 10 minutes or until golden. Serve warm or cooled. Makes 36 pieces.

Floating Kidneys

No need to seek out organ donors to make this freaky Kidney Bean Salad.

PREP: 15 minutes
CHILL: 4 to 24 hours

INGREDIENTS

- 1 16-ounce can cut wax beans or black beans, rinsed and drained
- 1 8-ounce can cut green beans or lima beans, rinsed and drained
- 1 8-ounce can red kidney beans, rinsed and drained
- ½ cup chopped green sweet pepper
- ⅓ cup chopped red onion
- ¼ cup vinegar
- 2 tablespoons sugar
- 2 tablespoons salad oil
- ½ teaspoon celery seeds
- ½ teaspoon dry mustard
- 1 clove garlic, minced

INSTRUCTIONS

In a large bowl, combine wax beans or black beans, green beans or lima beans, red kidney beans, sweet pepper, and red onion.

For dressing, in a screw-top jar combine vinegar, sugar, oil, celery seeds, dry mustard, and garlic. Cover and shake well. Pour over vegetables; gently stir. Cover and chill for at least 4 hours or up to 24 hours, stirring often. Makes 6 (side dish) servings.

Sharp Elbows

Clear a spot on the buffet for classic Macaroni Salad—or be prepared to take an elbow or two.

PREP: 30 minutes
CHILL: 4 to 24 hours

INGREDIENTS

- 1 cup elbow macaroni (3 ounces)
- ¾ cup cubed cheddar or American cheese (3 ounces)
- ½ cup thinly sliced celery (1 stalk)
- ½ cup frozen peas
- ½ cup thinly sliced radishes
- 2 tablespoons thinly sliced green onion or chopped onion
- ½ cup mayonnaise or salad dressing
- ¼ cup sweet or dill pickle relish, or chopped sweet or dill pickles
- 2 tablespoons milk
- 2 tablespoons horseradish mustard (optional)
- ¼ teaspoon salt
- Dash black pepper
- 2 hard-cooked eggs, coarsely chopped

INSTRUCTIONS

Cook the pasta according to package directions. Drain pasta. Rinse with cold water; drain again. In a large bowl combine cooked pasta, cheese, celery, peas, radishes, and onion.

For dressing, in a small bowl stir together mayonnaise, pickle relish, milk, mustard (if desired), salt, and pepper.

Pour the dressing over the pasta mixture. Add chopped eggs. Toss lightly to coat. Cover and chill for 4 to 24 hours. Before serving, if necessary, stir in additional milk to moisten. Makes 6 (side dish) servings.

Strained Brain

Guests won't have to think twice about whether they'd like a serving of this Shrimp Aspic.

PREP: 25 minutes
CHILL: 5 hours

INGREDIENTS

- 3 pounds frozen cooked medium shrimp (with tails), thawed and drained well
- ¼ cup roasted red sweet peppers, cut into ¼-inch-wide strips
- 1 cup chicken broth
- 1 teaspoon unflavored gelatin
- 1½ teaspoons finely shredded lemon peel
- ¼ cup lemon juice
- 3 tablespoons tomato paste
- 1 tablespoon honey
- 3 cloves garlic, minced
- ½ teaspoon salt
- ½ teaspoon ground ginger
- ¼ teaspoon cayenne pepper

INSTRUCTIONS

In a 1½ quart glass bowl (3 inches high, 7½-inches in diameter), begin arranging shrimp, tails toward the center, in a circle to make one flat layer in the bottom of the bowl. (Turn the shrimp so only the round backs are visible from the outside of the bowl.) Repeat layers until bowl is full, pressing down every couple of layers. As the bowl fills, tuck strips of roasted red peppers in and around the shrimp to form "blood vessels." (It helps to peer through the sides of the bowl to adjust as necessary.) When bowl is full, press down firmly with a plate that fits inside the bowl. Set aside.

In a small saucepan, combine chicken broth and unflavored gelatin; let stand 5 minutes. Cook and stir over medium heat until gelatin has dissolved. Whisk in lemon peel, lemon juice, tomato paste, honey, garlic, salt, ginger, and cayenne pepper until combined. Pour mixture over shrimp in bowl. Cover and chill at least 5 hours or overnight.

To unmold, set bowl for several seconds in a sink filled with warm water. Invert a large plate with sides over the bowl. Invert plate and bowl together and remove bowl to unmold. Cover and chill until needed (up to 24 hours). Makes 12 appetizer servings.

Bleeding Brie Heart

The raspberries give Raspberry Brie, a warm and cheesy puff pastry appetizer, its bloody appearance.

PREP: 20 minutes
BAKE: 20 to 25 minutes
STAND: 10 minutes

INGREDIENTS

- ½ 17.3-ounce package frozen puff pastry, thawed (1 sheet)
- ½ cup chopped pecans
- ⅓ cup raspberries
- 2 tablespoons honey
- 2 4½-ounce rounds Brie cheese
- 1 egg
- 1 tablespoon water
- Apple slices, pear slices, and/or seedless grapes

INSTRUCTIONS

Preheat oven to 375°F. Line a baking sheet with parchment paper; set aside.

Unfold pastry on a lightly floured surface; roll into a 16×10-inch rectangle. Cut two 8-inch circles from the pastry rectangle; reserve trimmings.

In a small bowl, combine pecans, raspberries, and honey. Divide raspberry mixture between the pastry circles, spooning mixture into the very center of each circle. Place Brie rounds on top of the raspberry mixture. Press down to spread mixture. Bring pastry up around Brie to enclose it, pleating and pinching edges to cover and seal. Cut off any excess pastry. Place, sealed side down, on prepared baking sheet.

In a small bowl, beat egg and water with a fork; set aside.

Using a fluted pastry wheel or small cookie cutters, cut reserved trimmings into decorative shapes, if desired. Brush egg mixture onto wrapped Brie; top with pastry shapes and brush again.

Bake for 20 to 25 minutes or until pastry is deep golden brown. Let stand for 10 minutes before serving. Serve with fruit. Makes 12 servings.

Icky Intestines

Even with a not-so-appetizing Halloween name, guests will gobble up Barbecue Sausages. They're a party staple!

PREP: 10 minutes
COOK: 4 to 5 hours (low) or 2 to 2½ hours (high)

INGREDIENTS

- 1 cup bottled barbecue sauce
- 1 16-ounce can jellied cranberry sauce
- 2 1-pound packages cocktail wieners and/or small cooked smoked sausage links

INSTRUCTIONS

In a 3½- or 4-quart slow cooker, stir together the barbecue sauce and cranberry sauce until combined. Stir in the wieners and/or sausages.

Cover and cook on low-heat setting for 4 to 5 hours or on high-heat setting for 2 to 2½ hours. Serve immediately or keep warm on low-heat setting for up to 2 hours. Serve with a slotted spoon or toothpicks. Makes 32 servings.

Rattling Rib Cage

With protruding bones, Standing Rib Roast is in prime form for a sinister buffet.

PREP: 10 minutes
ROAST: 1 hour 45 minutes
STAND: 15 minutes

INGREDIENTS

- 1 4- to 6-pound beef rib roast
- Salt and black pepper

INSTRUCTIONS

Season meat with salt and pepper. Place meat, fat side up, in a 15½×10½×2-inch roasting pan. Insert an oven-safe meat thermometer into center of roast, making sure it doesn't touch bone. Roast, uncovered, in a 350°F oven.

For medium rare, roast for 1¾ to 2¼ hours or until meat thermometer registers 135°F. Cover with foil; let stand 15 minutes. Temperature of meat after standing should be 145°F. For medium, roast for 2¼ to 2¾ hours or until meat thermometer registers 150°F. Cover; let stand 15 minutes. Temperature of meat after standing should be 160°F.

Makes 12 to 16 4-ounce servings.

Roasted Rump

Classic French Dip Sandwiches hit the spot on a cold and dark fall night.

PREP: 20 minutes
COOK: 9 to 10 hours (low) or 4½ to 5 hours (high)

INGREDIENTS

- 1 large sweet onion (such as Vidalia, Maui, or Walla Walla), cut into ½-inch-thick slices and separated into rings (1 cup)
- 1 2- to 2½-pound fresh beef brisket or boneless beef bottom round roast
- 2 cloves garlic, minced
- 1 teaspoon dried thyme, marjoram, or oregano, crushed
- ½ teaspoon black pepper
- 1¼ cups lower-sodium beef broth
- ½ cup water
- 1 tablespoon Worcestershire sauce
- 1 medium red or green sweet pepper, sliced
- 1 16-ounce loaf whole grain baguette-style bread, cut crosswise into 6 pieces and halved lengthwise, or 6 whole grain hoagie buns, split, and, if desired, toasted

INSTRUCTIONS

Place the onion rings in a 3½- to 5-quart slow cooker.

Trim separable fat from beef. If necessary, cut beef to fit into cooker. Place beef on top of the onions in the slow cooker. Sprinkle the beef with garlic, thyme, and pepper. Pour the beef broth, water, and Worcestershire sauce over all.

Cover and cook on low-heat setting for 9 to 10 hours for brisket or 8 to 9 hours for bottom round roast or on high-heat setting for 4½ to 5 hours for brisket or 4 to 4½ hours for bottom round roast.

Add red or green pepper to the slow cooker and allow to soften slightly. Transfer meat to a cutting board; thinly slice across the grain, removing any visible fat as you slice. Using a slotted spoon, remove onions and red pepper from cooker.

Divide sliced meat and onion and pepper slices among bread bottoms. Add bread tops.

Skim fat from cooking juices in cooker; pass juices for dipping sandwiches. Makes 6 servings.

Bleached Bones

Glazed Sweet Breads prove that bones can be oh so delectable—especially when brushed with icing.

PREP: 20 minutes
RISE: 20 minutes
BAKE: 15 minutes

INGREDIENTS

- 2 pounds frozen white bread dough, thawed
- 1⅓ cups powdered sugar
- 4 teaspoons butter, softened
- 4 to 6 teaspoons milk

INSTRUCTIONS

Grease two large baking sheets; set aside. Cut each loaf of dough into six pieces (12 pieces total).

Shape each piece into a 12-inch rope (let the dough rest as necessary while rolling). Using kitchen scissors, cut a V into the end of each dough rope to form the bone shape, rounding the ends as necessary.

Arrange breadsticks on the prepared baking sheets. Cover and let rise for 20 minutes.

Meanwhile, preheat oven to 375°F. Bake breadsticks for 15 to 20 minutes or until golden. Remove and cool on a wire rack.

For icing, in a small bowl stir together the powdered sugar, butter, and enough milk to make a thin icing.

Brush icing over all sides of cooled breadsticks. Allow to stand until icing sets. Makes 12 servings.

Graveyard Lady Fingers

The lady fingers conjure tombstones, but this Tiramisu is a sweet delight.

PREP: 30 minutes
CHILL: 6 hours

INGREDIENTS

- 30 crisp lady fingers (½ of a 17.64-ounce package)
- ½ cup brewed espresso or strong coffee
- 16 ounces mascarpone cheese
- 2 cups whipping cream
- ½ cup powdered sugar
- 2 teaspoons vanilla
- ⅓ cup chocolate liqueur
- 1 ounce bittersweet or semisweet chocolate, grated
- Chopped bittersweet or semisweet chocolate

INSTRUCTIONS

Line the bottom of a 2- to 2½-quart straight-sided clear dish with seven of the lady fingers, breaking to fit as necessary. Drizzle 3 tablespoons of the espresso over lady fingers; set aside.

In a large mixing bowl, beat together mascarpone cheese, whipping cream, powdered sugar, and vanilla with an electric mixer just until stiff peaks form. Beat in the chocolate liqueur until just combined. Spoon 2 cups of the mascarpone mixture over lady fingers in dish, spreading evenly. Brush 17* lady fingers lightly with 2 tablespoons of the espresso and arrange around the sides of the bowl, pressing into the mascarpone mixture lightly. Sprinkle grated bittersweet chocolate over the mascarpone mixture in the dish. Top with six more lady fingers, breaking to fit. Drizzle with remaining espresso. Top with remaining mascarpone mixture. Cover; chill for 6 to 24 hours. Sprinkle with chopped chocolate. Makes 16 servings.

** The number of lady fingers needed may vary with the width of the dish.*

Lace-Wrapped Pumpkins

MATERIALS

Black lace fabric
Pumpkin of any size
(We used Funkins.)
Needle and thread

INSTRUCTIONS

Lay the lace fabric over the pumpkin, gathering it at the bottom with your hand and marking the location for the stem opening. Remove the lace. Cut a small circle and lay the lace over the pumpkin, inserting the stem through the opening.

Gather the lace at the pumpkin bottom. Trim the excess lace, and secure the lace in place around the pumpkin using running stitches in a wheel-spoke pattern.

Spirit Panel

MATERIALS

2×3-foot birch ½-inch plywood panel
Manicure practice hand
Plastic mask
Crafts glue
Papier-mâché mix
(We used CelluClay.)
Spreader
Sandpaper
Latex paint and paintbrush

INSTRUCTIONS

Measure the bookshelf space and cut a plywood panel to size. Remove the back of the manicure hand with a bread knife.

Place mask and hand on the panel and glue in place, *photo 1.*

Prepare papier-mâché mix following the manufacturer's instructions.

With moist hands, add papier-mâché to the panel, *photo 2.* Spread the mixture, smoothing with the spreader. If your mask has open eye sockets, lay a damp piece of paper toweling over the openings and smooth the edges.

Allow the papier-mâché to dry slightly on the fingers before covering completely. When all the components are covered, let dry.

Save leftover mixture in an airtight bag for a light skim coat if necessary for a smooth finish. After all coats are dry, sand any rough edges or areas with sandpaper. Paint the panel to match the bookcase, *photo 3.* Let dry and slide into place.

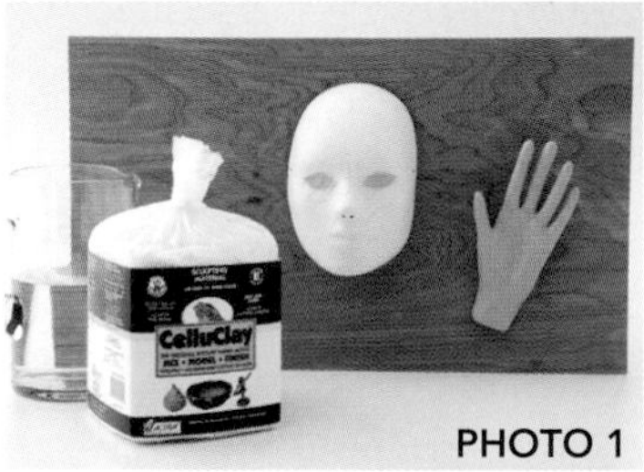

PHOTO 1

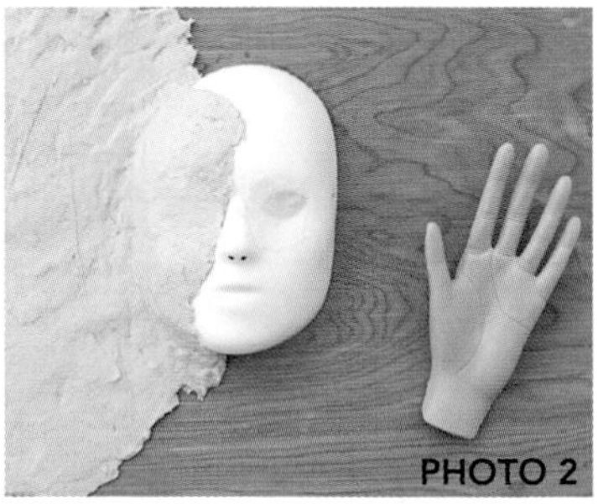

PHOTO 2

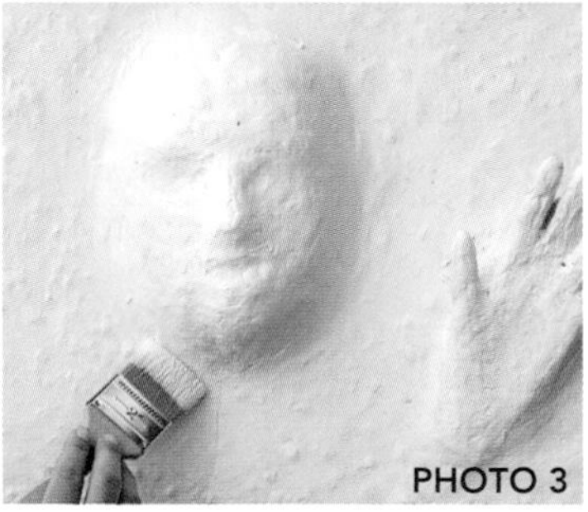

PHOTO 3

RIP Coffin

MATERIALS

Two 4×8-foot sheets of ½-inch plywood
Circular saw
8 yards of black felt
Rotary cutting tool
Wood glue
Finish nails
Staple gun and ½-inch staples
Two rolls of nickel nailhead trim
White chalk
Black acrylic crafts paint
Stencil brush

INSTRUCTIONS

Using the diagrams, *opposite,* and a pencil, tape measure, and straightedge, measure and mark all pieces for the coffin on the plywood sheets. Cut the pieces with the circular saw. Cut 1-inch wood cleats from the wood scraps.

Lay the bottom piece of the coffin on the black felt, and using the rotary cutting tool cut the felt along the outline of the bottom.

Assemble the coffin. Nail 1-inch wood cleats to the inner sides of the coffin at the height you want the bottom to rest. Glue

PHOTO A

PHOTO B

PHOTO C

the side panels at the corners and secure with nails. Insert the bottom piece on top of the cleats and secure with glue and nails.

Roll the remainder of the felt yardage along the sides of the coffin. Starting at a corner and smoothing with your hands as you go, staple the felt to the inside bottom edges of the coffin and the bottom outside edge, *photo A*. Leaving 2 inches of fabric on the edges, cut off remaining fabric from the bottom and inside. Lay the bottom felt shape in the coffin. Glue the felt to the board.

Attach nailhead trim along the top and bottom outside edges of the coffin, *photo B*. Add a vertical strip of trim about 1½ inches from both sides of each corner.

Photocopy the RIP letter pattern, *below,* enlarging to fit. Rub chalk on the back. Lay the pattern in place and go over the pattern lines with a pencil. Remove the pattern; pound nailheads in place on the pattern lines, referring to the pattern. Brush off excess chalk dust.

Squirt a small dot of black crafts paint onto a paper plate or paper towel. Dab a dry stencil brush into the paint and brush the excess onto the plate or paper towel. Stipple black paint onto the nailhead trim for an aged patina, *photo C.* Wipe off excess; let dry.

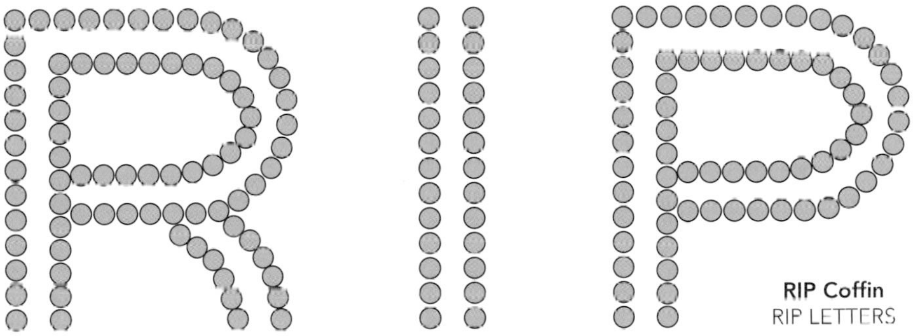

RIP Coffin
RIP LETTERS

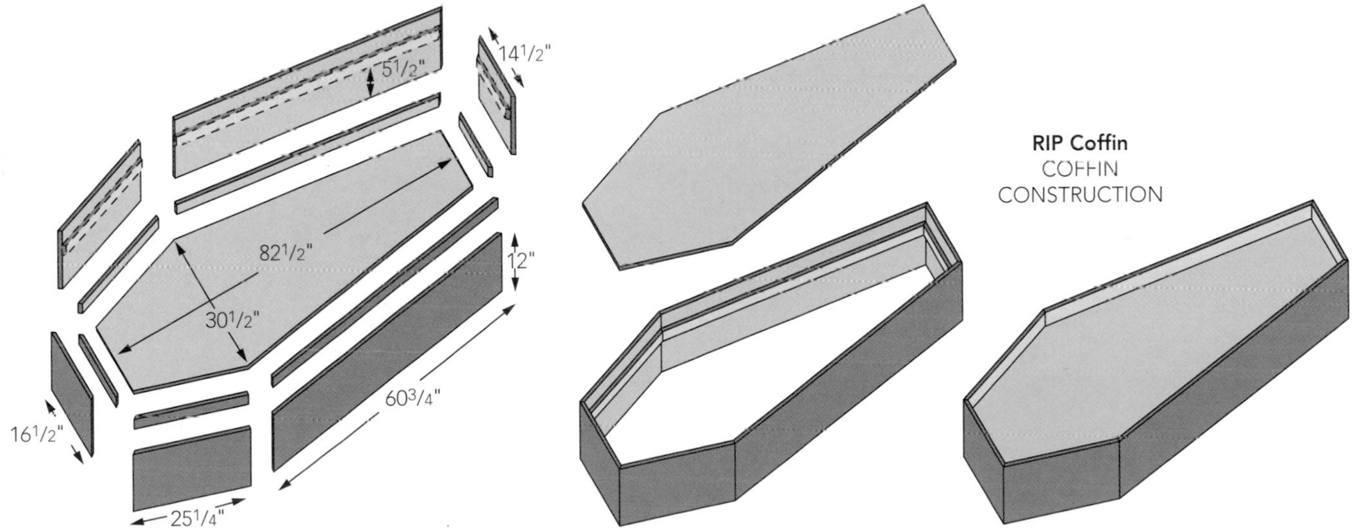

RIP Coffin
COFFIN CONSTRUCTION

party on!
Just copy, print, trim, and assemble to host a fall party filled with trick-or-treating ghosts, screech owls, friendly spiders, and colorful candy corn.

wicked-easy HALLOWEEN PARTY

Plan your party in minutes by letting us do the work for you. Set the stage with delightful printables designed by The Celebration Shoppe.

WRITTEN BY **DEBRA STEILEN**
PHOTOGRAPHY BY **MARTY BALDWIN**
STYLING INSPIRED BY **KIM M. BYERS**

Project instructions and patterns begin on *page 74*.

Look around your home for other ways to use the printables for party decor. For example, wrap pillar candles with the bottle labels for a quick change.

show your colors
A pennant-style banner, *right,* brings the party room to life. Candy corn, ghost, and screech owl motifs—as well as crisp stripes—make the paper creation a visual treat.

what a hoot
Lucky guests will easily find their way to the party after receiving such a sweetly spooky invitation, *opposite.* Send the invites out two to three weeks in advance to get maximum attendance—and to allow time for guests to scare up a costume.

stylish sippers
Turn orange soft drinks, *above left,* into a favorite fright-night refresher. Just copy, print, and trim our screech owl beverage wrappers and tape to the bottles.

center of attention
Anchor your dessert spread, *above,* with a yummy layer cake adorned with candy-corn cookies. Coordinated cupcake picks and a cute mini banner make it a special centerpiece.

pick your favorite
Festive paper wrappers and coordinating cupcake picks, *this photo*, take plain cupcakes to a new level. If you're pressed for time, simply transfer purchased cupcakes into the wrappers. Place on small plates on a tray for serving (and eating) ease.

costumed candy
Disguise chocolate candy bars, *above left,* for Halloween by wrapping them in bright paper, then adding one of our coordinated printables. Make all the bars look the same, or vary the papers and ribbon for a more colorful display.

clearly colorful
For a fast addition to your dessert table, just attach our tag designs to beribboned apothecary jars, *above.* Fill at will with your favorite Halloween-hue candy.

lollipop stand
Fool guests into thinking you spent hours decorating lollipops, *left,* when you really started with cellophane-wrapped pops and just added a copied and printed motif to each one. Display the finished lollipops in clear glass containers filled with white jelly beans.

"Whimsical adornments make party treats look even more tempting. Save time by starting with purchased confections. We promise not to tell!"

—KIM BYERS, THE CELEBRATION SHOPPE
THECELEBRATIONSHOPPE.COM

festive favor boxes
Colorful take-home gifts start with plain purchased take-out boxes, *opposite*. You add the Halloween personality with our copied and printed images, crepe paper, and ribbon.

pick-up-and-go popcorn
No bowls needed! Simply copy, print, trim, and twist our clever candy-corn cone pattern. Join the edges of the cone with tape and fill to the brim with another type of corn, *above*.

easy halloween eats
Tempt mummies, daddies, and all your ghoulish guests with piles of candy corn, *above*, in a coordinated container. Just wrap ribbon around a glass bowl and add one of our tag designs.

Go to **BHG.com/HTTbookwickedeasy** to print the free designs for these projects directly from your computer.

What a Hoot Invitation

MATERIALS

Invitation design, *below*
5×7-inch white cardstock

INSTRUCTIONS

Photocopy the invitation on white cardstock.

On a computer, create the text you want to use for party information on the invitation.

Format the text so it will fit within the gray area of the invitation. Run the invitation designs through your printer to overprint the text on the printed cardstock.

Show Your Colors Pennant-Style Banner

MATERIALS

Pennant designs, *opposite*
White cardstock
Crafts knife and straightedge or paper cutter
¼-inch-wide ribbon
Double-sided tape

INSTRUCTIONS

Enlarge and photocopy the five pennant designs on white cardstock; make multiples as desired to achieve necessary banner length. Trim carefully using a crafts knife and straightedge or a paper cutter. Cut ribbon long enough to drape across where you plan to hang the finished banner.

Arrange the individual pennants in the order you want them to appear on the finished banner. Attach the pennants to the ribbon with double-sided tape, folding the top edge of each pennant over the ribbon about ¼ inch. The top corners of the neighboring pennants should touch. Hang as desired.

What a Hoot Invitation

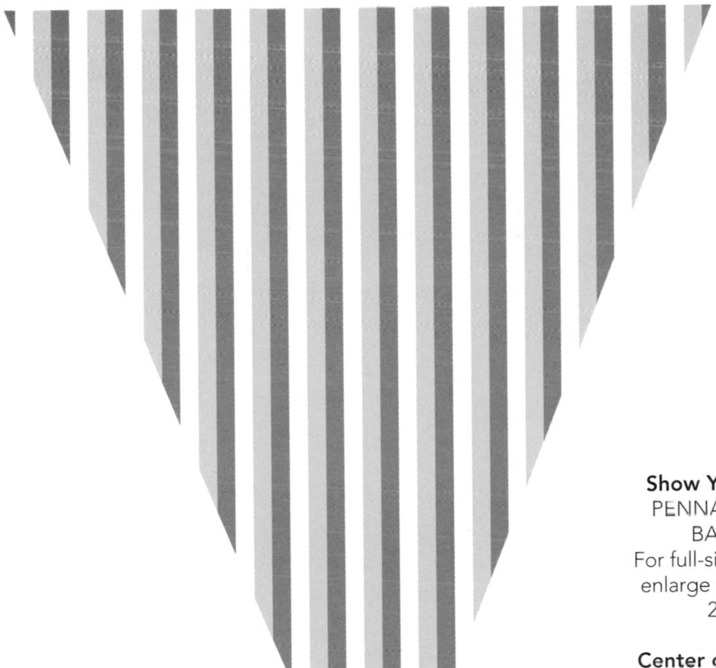

Show Your Colors
PENNANT-STYLE BANNER
For full-size pennants, enlarge each design 200%.

Center of Attention
CAKE MINI BANNER
For cake mini pennants, reduce each design to 25%.

Stylish Sippers BOTTLE LABEL Adjust size to fit bottle.

Stylish Sippers

MATERIALS

Bottle label, *left*
Crafts knife and straightedge or paper cutter
Double-sided tape

INSTRUCTIONS

Photocopy the desired number of bottle labels, and trim the edges using a crafts knife and straightedge or a paper cutter. Allow extra length for overlapping. Cover each bottle's logo with a printed label, using double-sided tape to secure.

Center of Attention Cake

MATERIALS

Pennant designs, *page 75*
White paper
Crafts knife or scissors
1 foot of white yarn
Crafts glue
White-frosted round layer cake
Candy-corn-shape sugar cookies
Orange-coated chocolate candies
3 completed cupcake picks (See instructions, *right*.)
2 bamboo skewers

INSTRUCTIONS

Reduce pennant images to 25 percent, and photocopy the desired number of mini pennants on white paper. Cut out. Glue the mini pennants to the white yarn; let dry. Attach a second pennant to the back of each pennant for a two-sided look.

Embed candy-corn-shape cookies around the side of the cake, alternating the cookie placement as shown, *below left*. Arrange orange-coated chocolate candies around the cake base. Insert the three cupcake picks on the cake top. Insert skewers on either side of the three picks. Tie the yarn with the mini pennants to the skewers to create a banner; dab each knot with crafts glue.

Pick Your Favorite Picks & Wrappers

MATERIALS

Cupcake pick and wrapper images, *opposite*
White paper
2½-inch circle punch
2-inch scalloped-circle punch
3-D adhesive dots (We used Pop Dots.)
Crafts knife
Wooden stir sticks
Double-sided tape
Scalloped-edge scissors

INSTRUCTIONS

Photocopy cupcake pick images on white paper. Use the circle punch to punch background tags. Use the scalloped-circle punch to punch smaller center tags. Attach each center tag to a large background tag with a 3-D adhesive dot. Cut wooden stir sticks to desired lengths. Attach one completed tag to each side of each stick using double-sided tape.

Photocopy cupcake wrapper images on white paper. Cut the convex side (the outside curve) of the wrapper shape with scalloped-edge scissors and all other edges, including the concave side, using a crafts knife or scissors. Assemble by overlapping the short edges to fit the baked cupcakes securely; adhere wrappers with double-sided tape. Slip a frosted cupcake inside each assembled wrapper. Embellish with a cupcake pick.

Pick Your Favorite
CUPCAKE PICKS

Pick Your Favorite
CUPCAKE WRAPPERS

Costumed Candy

MATERIALS

Orange paper
Full-size candy bars
Cupcake pick images, *page 77*
White paper
2-inch scalloped-edge circle punch
Double-sided tape
1¾-inch-wide black crepe paper
¼-inch-wide black-and-white striped ribbon or decorative paper

INSTRUCTIONS

Determine the size of the paper wrapper by carefully removing the original candy bar wrapper and measuring its height and width. Add ½ inch to the height. Using the resulting measurements, trim orange paper to size for each candy bar.

Photocopy the cupcake pick images on white paper. Use the 2-inch scalloped-edge circle punch to punch the images into tags.

Remove the original wrappers from the remaining candy bars, leaving silver foil liners. Wrap the orange paper around each bar, overlapping in back and taping in place. Using the photo, *above*, as a guide, add more decorations in the form of black crepe paper and striped ribbon or paper, attaching each piece with double-sided tape. Attach a tag to the center of each wrapped candy bar (atop the ribbon) with double-sided tape.

Festive Favor Boxes

MATERIALS

Cupcake pick images, *page 77*
White paper
2½-inch circle punch
2-inch scalloped-edge circle punch
3-D adhesive dots (We used Pop Dots.)
1¾-inch-wide crepe paper strips: black and orange
Translucent plastic wire-handle take-out boxes: 4×3×4 inches
Crafts glue
Double-sided tape
1-inch-wide black-and-white-polka-dot grosgrain ribbon
String or yarn
Black-and-orange dinner-size paper napkins

INSTRUCTIONS

Photocopy cupcake pick images on white paper. Use the 2½-inch circle punch to punch background tags. Use 2-inch scalloped-edge circle punch to cut out center tags. Attach each center tag to a large background tag with a 3-D adhesive dot.

Being careful not to cut all the way through the strip, embellish the orange crepe paper strip by making ½-inch cuts on each side toward the center, ¼ inch apart, with scissors. Cut lengths of the strip long enough to fit around the middle of the take-out boxes. Using the photo, *above*, as a guide, adhere a double layer of the snipped crepe paper around each box using crafts glue. Tape one of the completed medallions to the center of the strip at the front of each box.

To adorn the wire handles of the takeout boxes, cut grosgrain ribbon into 7-inch strips and tie one strip onto each handle with a single knot.

For each pom-pom, stack eight 4-inch lengths of black crepe paper. Snip the short ends every ¼ inch, cutting about 1½ inches toward the center. Wrap a short piece of string or yarn around the middle of the stack, gathering to create the pom-pom. Tie a knot in the string or yarn; use the free ends to tie a pom-pom around the handle of each take-out box.

Line the inside of each embellished take-out box with a dinner-size paper napkin. Fill the decorated box with treats before securing the box top. Lift the wire handle so the pom-poms and bows are displayed.

Pick-Up-and-Go Popcorn Cones

MATERIALS

Popcorn cone image, *opposite*
White cardstock
Crafts knife or scissors
Double-sided tape

INSTRUCTIONS

Photocopy the desired number of candy-corn cones on white cardstock; cut out. Fold under the tabbed edge at the dotted line. Twist each printed cone shape until the folded tab fits under the opposite edge. Adhere with double-sided tape. Fill with popcorn and nestle in a bed of candy to hold upright.

Easy Halloween Eats

MATERIALS

Food label image, *below*
White paper
Crafts knife and straightedge or paper cutter
½-inch-wide ribbon or decorative paper
Clear candy dishes and jars
Double-sided tape

INSTRUCTIONS

Note: Go to BHG.com/HTTbookwickedeasy for a full set of free labels complete with preprinted food names.

Photocopy the food label image on white paper, making enough for all the dishes and jars to be labeled. Trim labels using a crafts knife and straightedge or a paper cutter. Cut a length of ribbon or decorative paper long enough to fit around the candy dish, with enough extra to overlap ends. Wrap the ribbon or paper around the candy dish and tape in place. Attach a food label to the ribbon or paper, covering the overlapped ends.

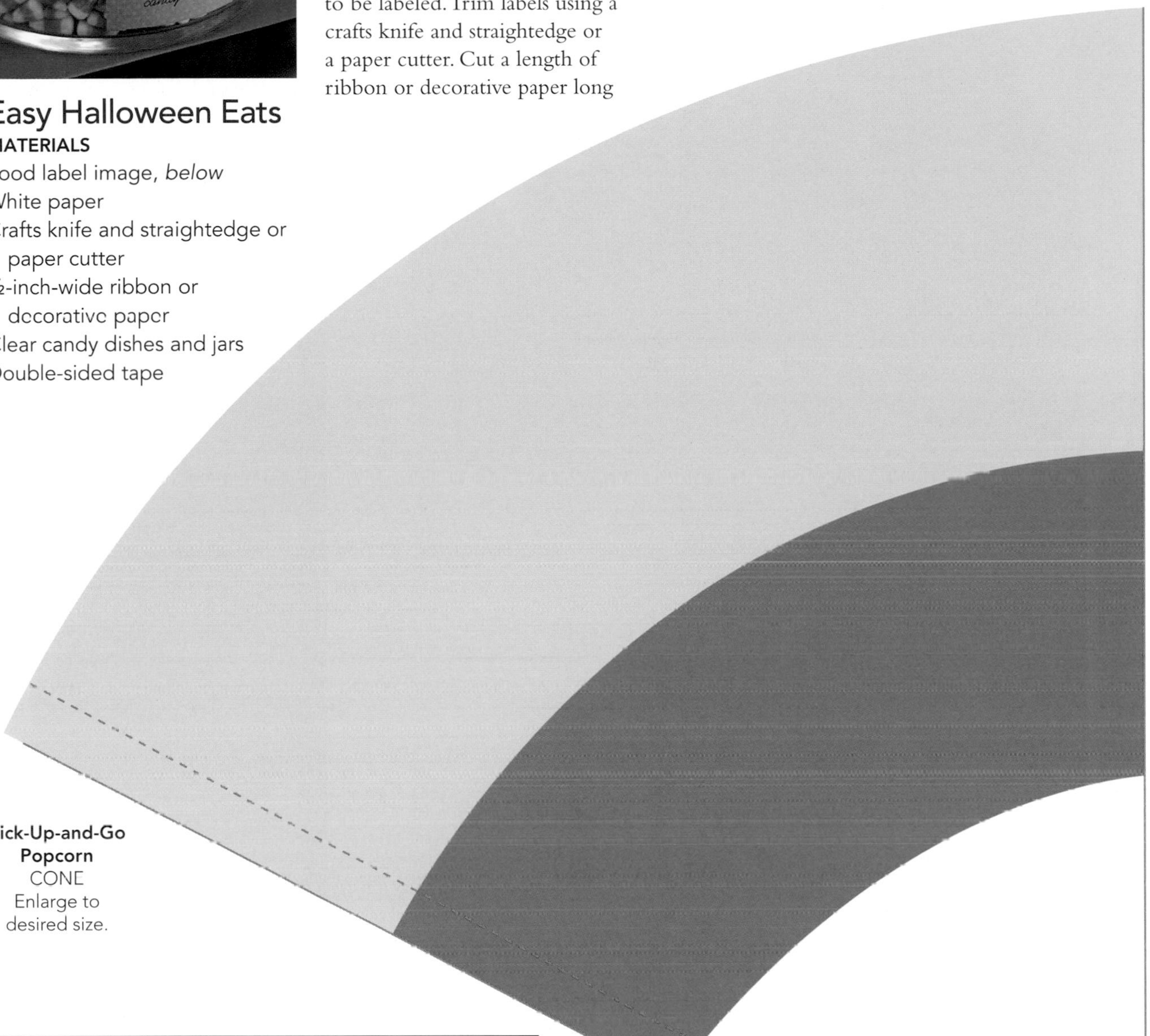

Pick-Up-and-Go Popcorn CONE
Enlarge to desired size.

Easy Halloween Eats LABEL   Adjust size as desired.

Monster Bash

Here's how to throw a not-so-spooky shindig featuring gentle giants, a beastie-bites buffet, and flights-of-fancy amusements designed to please your favorite little ones.

DESIGNED BY **CARRIE NAUMANN** WRITTEN BY **ANN WILSON** PHOTOGRAPHY BY **JAY WILDE**
CUPCAKES AND POPS PROVIDED BY **WILTON ENTERPRISES**

Project instructions and patterns begin on *page 88*.

banner day

Suspend spirited signage, indoors or out, to highlight your friendly-fiend theme and pepped-up color scheme. Tuck quirky paper critters behind glass cabinet doors or hang them on walls for "pin the horns on a monster" competitions.

Traditional Halloween parties, packed with gruesome displays of ghouls and goblins, can be way too scary for tiny tykes. We devised a kinder, gentler party plan for preschoolers that substitutes fanciful monster figures for more fearsome forms and employs cheerful chroma in place of horror-inducing hues.

A perky palette of bright lime, aqua, pink, and sherbet orange and playful patterns create an upbeat atmosphere and bright-and-breezy backdrops. The energetic scheme pops up again and again. Invitations, grinning monsters, party games, take-home favors, and ogre-inspired edibles spill over with lighthearted attitude, comical character, and a few trick-or-treat surprises.

Follow our lead (or adapt our ideas to suit your entertaining needs) and build a fun-filled and very festive afternoon around making nice-monster motifs. We supply you with the templates, patterns, and projects—plus the inspiration and instructions—you'll need to stage a monstrously pleasing Halloween gathering that instills smiles over screams.

masked marauders
Put imaginations into play. Supply kids with a pile of handmade puzzle pieces, *above,* and watch as they puzzle the pieces into instant disguises.

puzzle me this
Keep little hands busy with impishly imaged puzzles, *opposite left,* crafted from monster portraits and balsa wood. Make a puzzle for every guest to carry home as a playtime keepsake.

who's scaring whom?
Craft amiably expressive monsters, *opposite right,* using polka-dot gift-wrap bodies, dimensional facial features cut from complementary papers, and computer-printed speech bubbles.

interactive invite
Attach a "me need fun!" bubble, *left,* with a brad so each invitee can swing it around to reveal the party-day essentials printed beneath.

request their presence
Preview monstrous pleasures and ensure maximum attendance by sending theme invites, *below,* two to three weeks ahead of the big day.

deep-blue-sea drink

Fill a large clear-glass fishbowl, *below,* with blue Gatorade, and add a gummy octopus with its tentacles trailing over the side. Float "looking at you" candy-dotted marshmallow eyeballs atop the aqua sea.

cyclops on sticks

Parade edible brownie pops—created using molds and decorated with icing, fondant, marshmallow, and licorice-strip details—across a tabletop, *below,* for a monstrously fun decoration and dessert. Display the kooky confections in rickrack-trimmed vases filled with plastic foam to hold the pops in place, marbles, and colorful blooms. Tie a gingham ribbon to each stick for a festive flourish.

uncanny eats

Gratifyingly gross, renamed candies and crudités, *above,* tempt tots' taste buds. Print made-up monikers, such as scales (jelly beans), fangs (candy corn), tentacles (pickle slices), and monster bones (carrot sticks), onto adhesive labels and adhere to serving pieces.

fetching finale
Pile a tiered tray, *this photo*, with funny-face cupcakes to fashion an appealing anchor for your good-eats tabletop. Use brightly colored icings, fondants, and store-bought candies to turn plain-Jane baked goods into sure-to-delight desserts.

personality-plus pictures
Print the coloring template, *page 92*, on 11×17-inch paper. Encourage marker-wielding artists to fill in the images with creative color combos, *this photo*. Dress your serving and creation stations with easy-clean toppers cut from oilcloth.

magnetic mementos

Capture every monster-in-the-making moment with a digital camera. Print images and insert them into preprinted magnetic frames, *left,* that guests can take home to post on their refrigerators as party souvenirs.

great pretenders

What kid doesn't love to act like a monster? Improvisational impersonators, *above*, can do just that—again and again—when you supply them with a pint-size platform and face-framing beastie boy and girl silhouettes.

Go to ***BHG.com/HTTbookmonster*** for free printable patterns and additional guides.

Magnetic Mementos

MATERIALS

Frame image, *page 92* or downloaded
Magnetic printer paper
Digital camera
Photo or printer paper
Clasp envelopes

INSTRUCTIONS

Print picture-frame template in color on sheets of magnetic printer paper; cut along scalloped edges and cut out frame centers. Write guests' names in label areas on frames. Take digital images of each guest. Print digital images on photo or printer paper. (We used an Epson PictureMate printer, which speeded up the process.) For each guest, place the desired image behind the frame and insert both pieces in a carry-home envelope.

Banner Day Bash Banner

MATERIALS

Solid and patterned scrapbook paper
Crafts glue
Chipboard letters
Paper hole punch
Grommets, two for each pennant
Ribbon

INSTRUCTIONS

On complementary paper, draw 7-inch-tall pennant-shape triangles. Make enough for the desired banner length. Use a lid or glass as a template to draw circles that will fit on the triangles. Cut out. Adhere contrasting circles to pennants, and glue chipboard letters atop circles to spell desired greeting. In the triangles' upper corners, punch holes to hold the grommets. Add the grommets. Cut a length of ribbon and string it through the grommets to hang the banner.

Interactive Invitations

MATERIALS

Invitation and monster patterns, *page 93* or downloaded
Scrapbook paper
Black permanent marker
Adhesive dots
Scrapbooking brads
Envelopes

INSTRUCTIONS

Cut invitation backgrounds from solid-color scrapbook paper. (Make sure invitations are properly sized to fit your mailing envelopes.) Photocopy "me need fun" speech bubbles and "come to my monster bash" panels onto white paper; cut out.

Photocopy and trace around monster template (adjust size if needed) or draw monsters freehand onto scrapbook paper. Or photocopy and cut out color monster pattern, *page 93*. Outline areas and add details with black marker. Cut out figures and use adhesive dots to adhere them to the invitations.

Write the party details on each "come to my monster bash" bubble, and adhere to each invitation with adhesive dots. Place "me need fun" bubble over party details and attach it with a brad so the panel can swing up to reveal what, when, and where.

Great Pretenders Photo-Op Figures

MATERIALS

Monster patterns, *below* or downloaded
Foam-core board
Acrylic paint
Paintbrushes
Black permanent marker
Crafts knife
Hot-glue gun and glue sticks

INSTRUCTIONS

Enlarge monster-body templates to your desired size. Use the downloadable guides for assistance, if needed. Trace all patterns onto foam-core board with pencil.

Paint all silhouettes. Let dry. Outline the painted areas and details using a black marker. Use a crafts knife to cut out the torsos, accessories, and body parts; cut away mouth areas to accommodate posing kids' faces. Hot-glue the body parts and accessories to the torsos. Hot-glue a foam-core triangle to the lower area of figures to create a stand to keep the monsters upright.

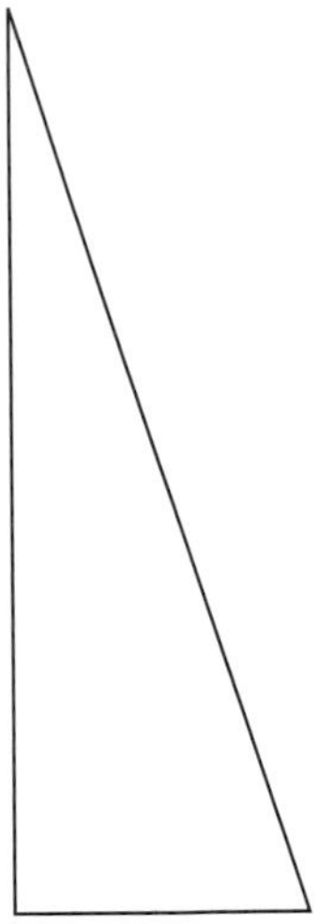

Puzzle Me This Monster Puzzles

MATERIALS

Monster images, *pages 94–95* or downloaded
Balsa wood
Crafts knife
Acrylic paint
Paintbrushes
Decoupage medium

INSTRUCTIONS

Photocopy the color monster images onto white paper. Cut out each image and use as a pattern to cut a balsa wood shape for each puzzle. Cut balsa wood and each printed image into three panels, as shown in the diagram, *page 95*. Paint all surfaces of balsa wood a color that coordinates with the image. Let dry.

Adhere and seal the images to the corresponding balsa wood pieces with decoupage medium.

Cyclops on Sticks Brownie Pops

MATERIALS

Silicone brownie mold (We used Wilton Brownie Pops silicone mold.)
Brownie mix
Buttercream frosting
White fondant
Tints: orange, rose, and black
Icing decorator tips: 1A, 1M, 1, 2, 8, and 12
Frosting brush
Piping gel
White sparkles
Disposable frosting decorating bags
8-inch lollipop sticks

INSTRUCTIONS

Note: Instructions are for pink-striped and pink-dotted brownie pops. For other brownie pop designs, go to BHG.com/HTTbookmonster *for instructions.*

Bake and cool brownies in prepared mold supported by a cookie sheet; carefully remove from mold. Lightly frost the pops smooth with buttercream frosting.

Polka-Dot Brownie: Tint fondant orange; roll out ⅛ inch thick. Cover pops in orange fondant. Roll out white and black fondant to ⅛ inch thick; cut out white of eye with wide end of tip 1M and cut black fondant pupil from narrow end of tip 1A. Cut an orange eyelid with a knife. Attach with a water-dampened brush. Tint fondant rose; roll out ⅛ inch thick; cut out rose dots using both ends of tip 12. Brush all dots with piping gel and cover with sparkles. Attach dots to body with a water-dampened brush. Pipe on black eyelashes with tip 2. Insert sticks.

Striped Brownie: Tint fondant light rose; roll out ⅛ inch thick. Cover pops with light rose fondant. Tint fondant dark rose; roll out ⅛ inch thick. Cut three ¼-inch-wide stripes in dark rose. Brush with piping gel and cover with sparkles. Attach stripes with a water-dampened brush. Cut out white eyes with wide end of tip 12. Cut black fondant pupils using narrow end of tip 8. Cut out eyelids with a knife. Attach eyes with a water-dampened brush. Pipe on black lashes with tip 2. Insert lollipop sticks.

Banner Day Cabinet Critters

MATERIALS

Monster-figure patterns, *right* or downloaded
Complementary wrapping and scrapbook papers
Black permanent marker
Crafts glue
Tape

INSTRUCTIONS

Enlarge and copy the monster-figure patterns to your desired size. Download guides for assistance, if needed. Trace the pattern pieces onto the back of wrapping and/or scrapbook papers. Cut out all pieces. Outline edges and add details with a black marker. Glue body pieces to the torsos; let dry. Tape the figures to glass-pane doors, windows, or walls.

Fetching Finale Cupcakes

MATERIALS

Muffin pan
Cake mix
Buttercream frosting
White fondant
Tints: orange, teal, rose, black, and leaf green
Icing decorator tips: 1A, 2, and 3
Disposable frosting decorating bags
Candy spearmint leaves
Frosting brush
Candy gumdrops: red
Granulated sugar

INSTRUCTIONS

Note: Instructions are for Ted and Alice cupcakes, shown far right and second from left. For instructions for remaining cupcake designs, go to BHG.com/HTTbookmonster.

Bake and cool cupcakes. Frost the cupcakes smooth with buttercream frosting, mounding up in center.

Ted Cupcake: Tint fondant orange, roll fondant 1/16 inch thick, and cover cupcake. Tint fondant teal, and shape into ears, arms, and nose; let dry. Roll white fondant 1/16 inch thick and cut out teeth. Insert arms, ears, nose, and teeth into cupcake. Cut out eyes using the wide end of tip 1A. Pipe pupils and eyebrows with tip 3. Roll spearmint leaves out on waxed paper sprinkled with sugar; cut into antler shapes with scissors dipped in sugar, and insert in place.

Alice Cupcake: To ensure that the fondant bow retains its shape, prepare and let dry for 48 hours. Tint fondant leaf green. Roll fondant 1/16 inch thick. Cut two $1\frac{1}{2}\times\frac{1}{4}$-inch strips. Fold ends toward the center and pinch ends together. Cut a $2\times\frac{1}{4}$-inch strip and notch a "V" on each end; let strips dry. Lay folded strips on top of the notched strip. Cut a $\frac{1}{4}\times1$-inch strip and wrap the center, flattening the ends on the back side.

Tint fondant rose. Roll fondant 1/16 inch thick and cover cupcake. Tint fondant black. Roll 1/16 inch thick; cut into a mouth shape. Attach with a water-dampened brush. Shape white fondant into eyeball shapes. Cut eyelids from rose-tinted fondant with a knife and press onto the eyes. Pipe pupils and eyelashes with tip 3. Roll white fondant 1/16 inch thick and cut out teeth. Cut a rose uvula with a knife. Attach the bow, eyes, teeth, and uvula with a water-dampened brush. Tint fondant orange and cut dots with tip 2. Attach with a water-dampened brush.

Roll gumdrops out on waxed paper sprinkled with sugar; cut into tongue shape with scissors dipped in sugar, score in the center, and insert in mouth.

Personality-Plus Pictures COLORING SHEET Enlarge 215% or to desired size.

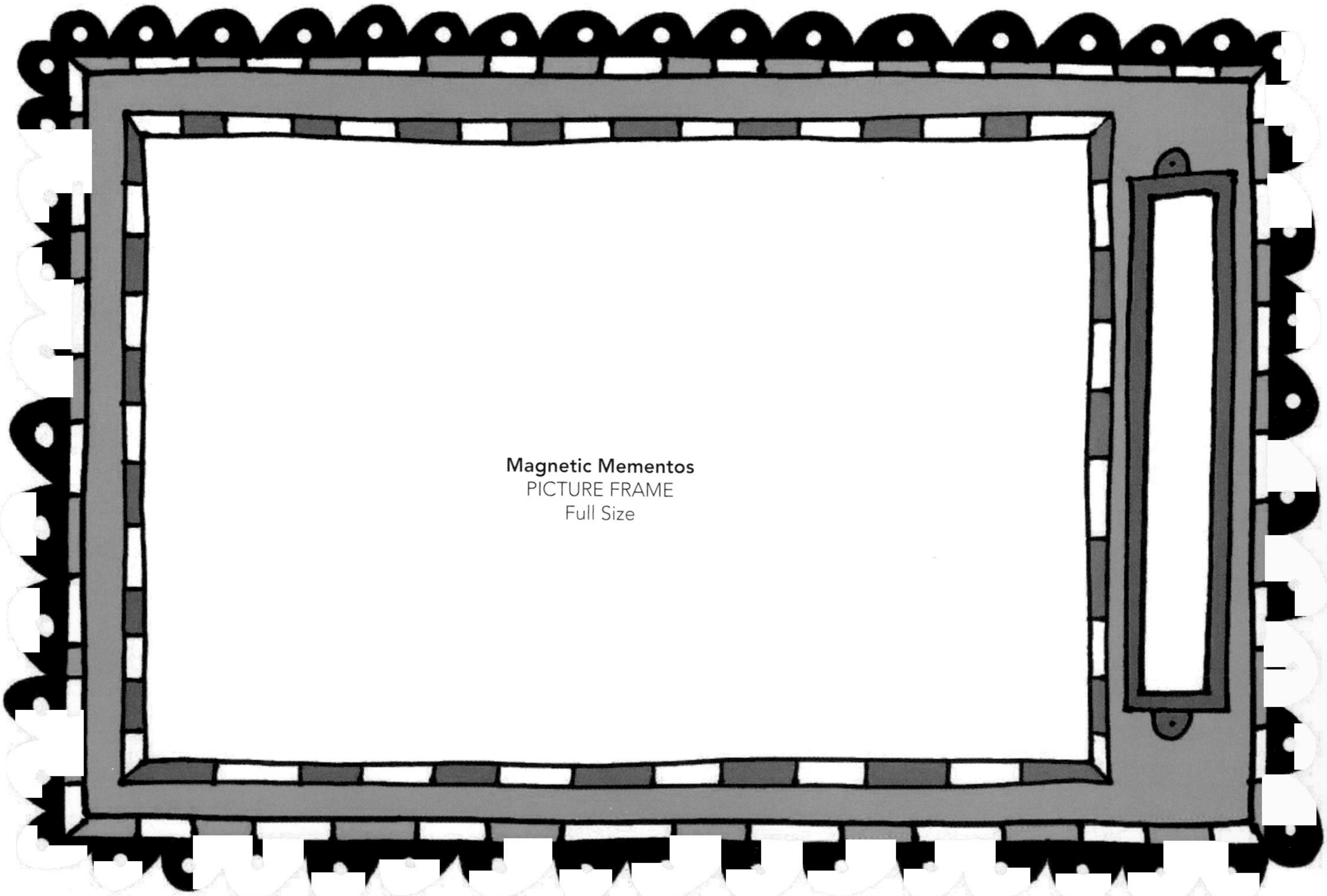

Magnetic Mementos
PICTURE FRAME
Full Size

me
need
fun!

come to my
monster bash!

Interactive Invitations PATTERNS & TEMPLATE
Adjust to desired size if necessary.

Puzzle Me This
MONSTER
PUZZLES
Full Size

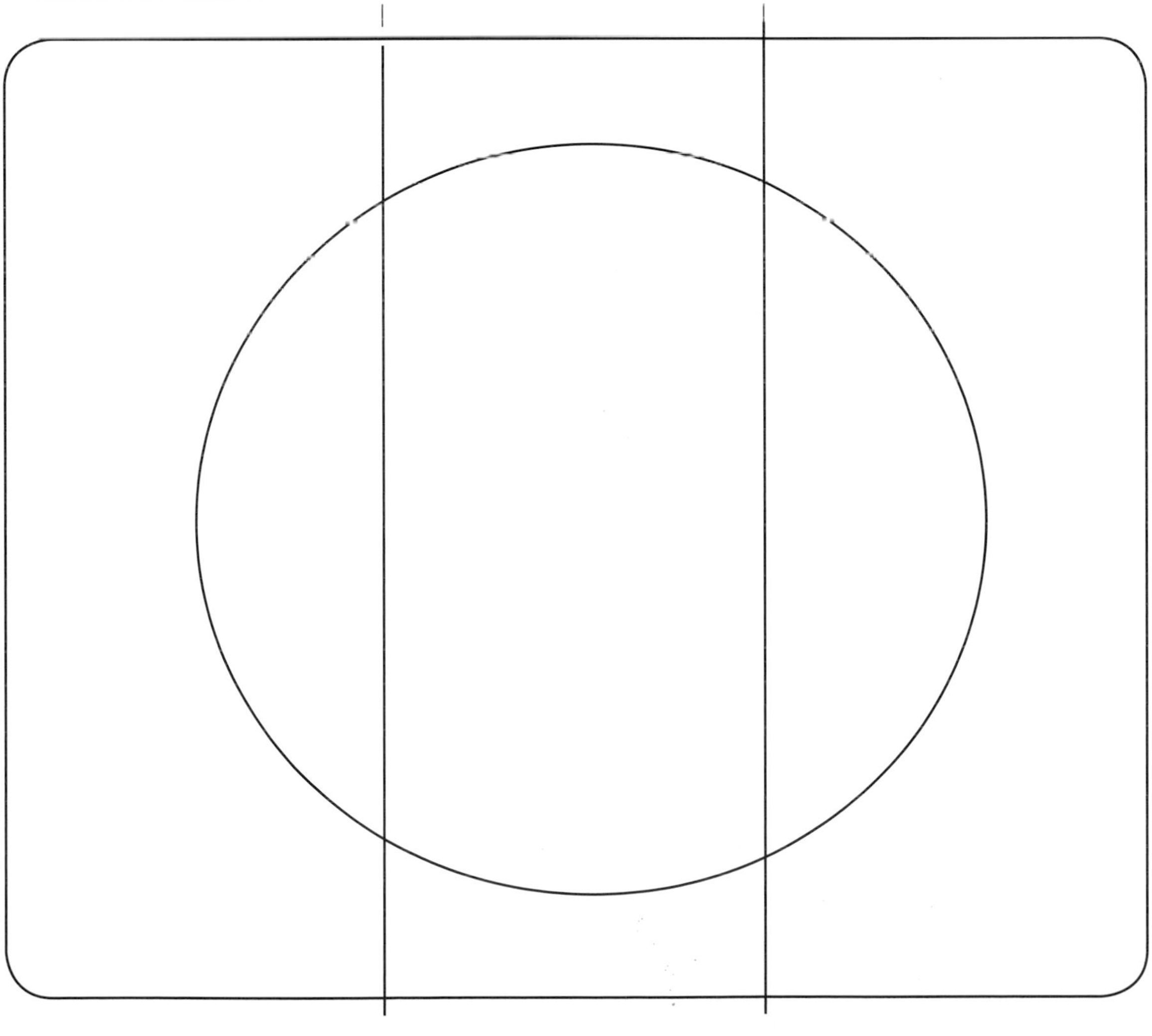

Puzzle Me This
MONSTER
PUZZLE
& DIAGRAM
Full Size

fright night INVITES

Tempt your friends to boo-gie by sending them one of these adorable Halloween party invitations. We dare them to send their regrets.

DESIGNED BY **CANDI GERSHON**
WRITTEN BY **ELIZABETH A. JENSEN**
PHOTOGRAPHY BY **JAY WILDE**

Project instructions and patterns begin on page 100.

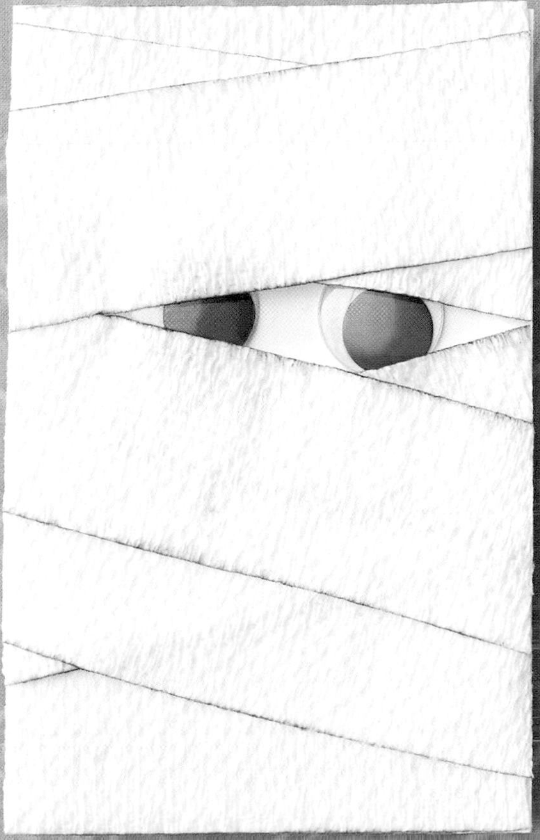

bubbling brew
Paper circles and buttons spill from this cauldron invite, *opposite*. Recipients will bubble over with excitement.

under wraps
Googly eyes gazing out from gauzy bandages make this mummy card, *above*, seem like the real deal.

freak show
Introduce your monster mash by sending this flip-top invite, *right*, to your nearest and eerie-est. Button eyes give the guy a crazed look.

Take your pick—scary or sweet! Either way, a fun invitation will get the party hopping.

vamp it up
There's a new vampire on the scene. This grinning guy, *left,* opens his cape to reveal a fang-tastic invitation.

ghost-est with the most-est
This adorable apparition, *below,* will inspire guests to float by. White vellum gives the ghostly appearance.

in the bag
Warning! Sending this invitation, *above,* may result in a mad rush of partygoers to your doorstep. The card pulls out of the mini paper bag to reveal an enticing appeal to play some tricks and enjoy many treats.

sweet treat
Summon friends with this candy-inspired invitation, *above right.* It's easy to make and a treat to receive.

scaredy-cats
The piercing green eye on this black cat, *right,* will catch guests' attention when you ask them over for some hair-raising fun.

Bubbling Brew

MATERIALS

Cardstock: gray and black
Adhesive
Crafts foam dots
Circle paper punches: ⅛-, ½-, ¾-inch-diameter
Solid and patterned paper
Assorted buttons
Cotton ball

INSTRUCTIONS

Fold an 11×7-inch piece of gray cardstock. Using the Bubbling Brew Cauldron pattern, *below*, cut out one complete cauldron from black cardstock. Cut a second rim-only pattern. Trace and cut one rim piece from black cardstock. Adhere the complete cauldron to the front of the card. Use crafts foam dots to glue the rim piece to the front of the card as shown, *page 96*.

Punch or cut about 15 circles in various sizes and patterns from paper. Adhere pieces of crafts foam to the backs of a few. Adhere circles and buttons to the cauldron, referring to the photo, *page 96* and *left*, for placement.

Pull a cotton ball into pieces, and adhere it to the card to resemble steam.

Print "Something's brewing…" onto solid paper. Cut out the strip, and attach it to the cauldron. Write or print party details on solid paper. Cut the paper to fit inside the invitation and adhere.

Under Wraps

MATERIALS

White cardstock
1-inch-diameter googly eyes
White gauze bandage
Black permanent marker
Adhesive

INSTRUCTIONS

Print invitation text on an 8×10-inch piece of cardstock, placing

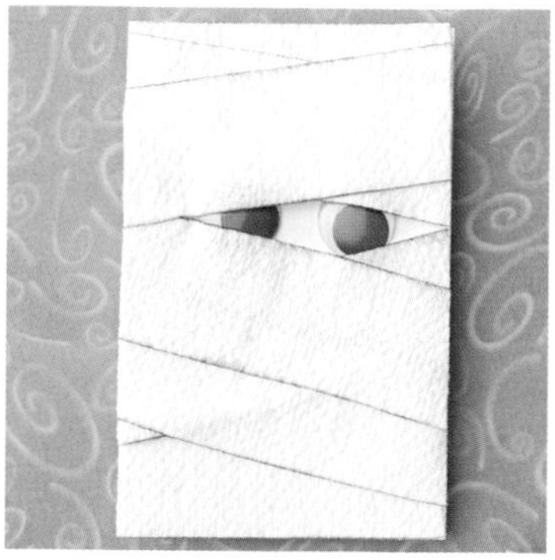

within the right-hand side of the horizontal sheet.

Fold cardstock in half. Adhere googly eyes to the front. Unwrap about 72 inches of gauze bandage, lay flat, and lightly mark the edges with black marker. Cut the bandage into 5-inch strips. Adhere to the card front. Continue until you've achieved the desired look. Trim the ends that overlap the edges.

Freak Show

MATERIALS

Cardstock: lime green, black, white, and silver
Adhesive
Buttons: two mismatched black; two smaller mismatched white
Sewing needle and black embroidery floss

INSTRUCTIONS

Cut a 6×11-inch piece of lime-green cardstock for the base of the invitation. Round the bottom corners with scissors. Fold the cardstock 3½ inches from the top to create a flap. Glue a 6×3½-inch piece of black cardstock to the folded edge. Cut triangular shapes to create hair.

Print your invitation details on white cardstock. Cut the white cardstock to fit inside the flap, and adhere it. Glue on black and white buttons to create eyes. Cut and adhere a strip of black cardstock for the monster's mouth. Sew on a scar with a needle and black embroidery floss. Adhere an 8×1-inch strip of silver cardstock to the card back to create bolts.

Vamp It Up

MATERIALS

Cardstock: black, green, red, and white
Red patterned paper
Adhesive
Googly eyes
Red button

INSTRUCTIONS

Using the patterns, *below*, cut cape, mouth, eyebrows, and hair from black cardstock. Cut the face from green cardstock, bow tie from red cardstock, teeth from white cardstock, and coat pieces from red patterned paper.

Print invitation details on a 4×7-inch piece of white cardstock. Assemble the vampire, and attach googly eyes. Adhere the red patterned and white pieces to the inside of the cape; fold cape sides to cover the white cardstock. Attach the red button to the outer flap.

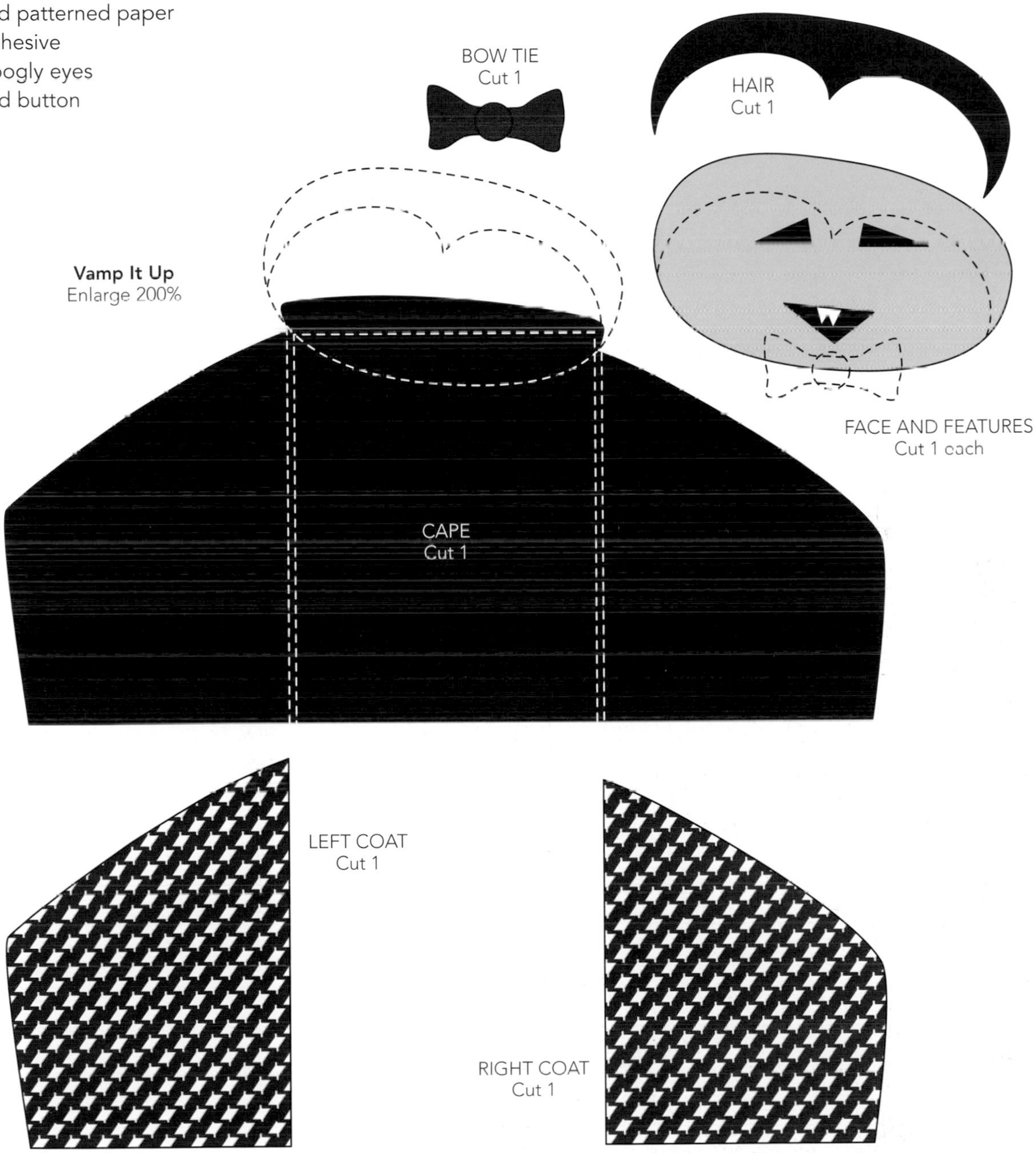

Ghost-est with the Most-est

MATERIALS

Cardstock: white and black
White vellum
Black permanent marker
Silver paint pen
Black-and-white ribbon
Small hole punch
Brad

INSTRUCTIONS

Print invitation information on white cardstock, fitting it within a 4×8-inch space. Using the Ghost-est with the Most-est pattern, *below*, cut one ghost from the printed white cardstock and one from vellum. Outline the white cardstock with a black marker. Outline the vellum with a silver paint pen.

Fold a small piece of ribbon into a bow as shown in the photo, *left*. Stack the ribbon, vellum, and white cardstock; punch a hole through the layers and secure all with a brad. Punch black cardstock circles for eyes, and adhere them to the vellum.

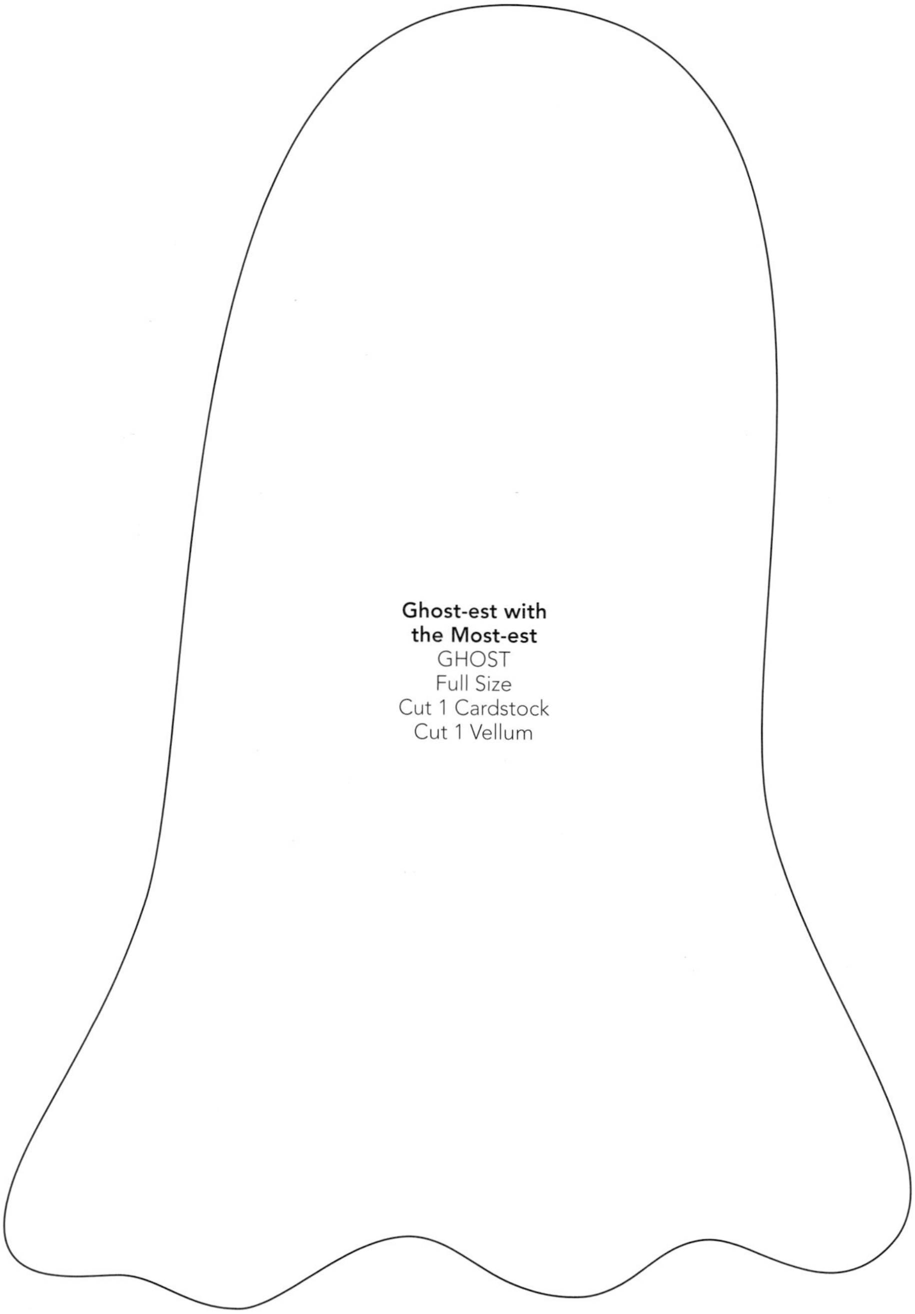

In the Bag

MATERIALS

Patterned paper
Cardstock: black and white
Adhesive
Rub-on letters
Die-cut candy designs
8-inch length of twine
Mini paper bag: 3½×6¾-inch
Circle punch: 2-inch-diameter

INSTRUCTIONS

Round the bottom corners of a 3¼×6¾-inch rectangle of patterned paper.

Print the party information on black cardstock. Center and glue the printed rectangle on the back of the invitation. Use rub-on letters or print "Trick or Treat" on patterned paper; cut out design and adhere it to the front of the invitation.

Glue a 1½-inch-wide strip of black cardstock to the top of the card. Glue die-cut candies and twine to the top of card as shown, *above*.

Insert the invitation in the paper bag and mark the location of the "Trick or Treat" design. Remove the invitation. Punch a circle from the front of the paper bag so the text will show.

Sweet Treat

MATERIALS

Cardstock: black, orange, yellow, and white
Adhesive

INSTRUCTIONS

Using the Sweet Treat pattern, *right*, cut black cardstock for the invitation base.

Print elements of the invitation text on white, orange, and yellow cardstock. Trim the printed pieces to fit each section as shown, and adhere to the base.

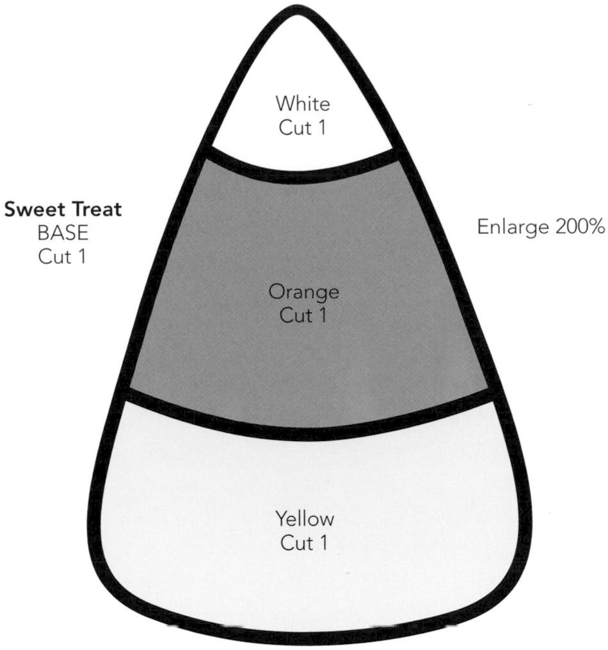

Scaredy-Cats

MATERIALS

Cardstock: black and white
Silver paint pen
Adhesive
Crafts foam
Green-and-black cat eye

INSTRUCTIONS

Using the Scaredy-Cats pattern, *right*, cut the cat from black cardstock. Place the cat on scrap paper, and trace the edges with a silver paint pen. Let dry.

Print the invitation details on white cardstock; cut into strips. Attach crafts foam to the back of the "No Scaredy-Cats Allowed!" strip, and adhere the text to the body of the cat. Glue the eye to the cat's face.

ultimate party guide

Ready to get your Halloween on? These kid-pleasing party ideas will help you weave a web of fun and happy high jinks for all little ghoul and goblin guests to enjoy. Choose a few projects or dig into the whole kit and ca-boo-dle.

cute-as-a-bug party set
Make a good first—and last—impression with a coordinated invitation and favor bag, *left*. The playful big-eyed bug ensemble is especially good for young children. The invitation promises not to bite, but the tooth-chomped corner indicates otherwise. Stenciled circles make it easy to coordinate the designs. A bug-face ring—a fun little extra—is easily made with a foam ball, googly eyes, and a chenille stem. Instructions are on *page 112*.

PARTY SET: DESIGNED BY SHERRIE RAGSDALE FOR PLAID. **TREAT BAG:** DESIGNED BY BRENDA PINNICK; PROVIDED BY ELLISON. **TREAT TOPPER:** PROVIDED BY ELLISON

sweet skeleton treat bag
This tiny bag, *left*, is sweet inside and out. To make one, photocopy the patterns on *page 113*. Use the patterns to cut the pieces from felt. Also from felt, cut a 2×4¼-inch black rectangle, two 5¾×7½-inch orange rectangles for the bag front and back, and a 3½×22-inch orange strip for the sides and bottom. Glue the design to the front, centering the black rectangle ¾ inch from the bottom edge. With wrong sides together and a ½-inch seam allowance, sew one long edge of the orange strip to the sides and bottom of front piece. Attach the back in the same way. Trim with pinking shears. Add ribbon handles.

Try a neighborhood party and spread the fun with a meal at one house and crafts, games, and storytelling at others.

jack-o'-lantern treat topper
Include an incognito treat at each place setting, or arrange dozens in a display to hand out at the end of the party. To make the topper, *right*, photocopy the patterns on *page 113*. Cut two of each shape from colored cardstock. Place the pumpkins on a surface, flipping one so it mirrors the other. Glue black paper over the face openings and attach the collar. On the opposite (front) side, add the hat. Glue a face to each side of a wrapped candy stick and finish with a bow tied at the neck.

the countdown

Your little ones are clamoring for a Halloween party, but you get the heebie-jeebies wondering how to pull it together. Don't go batty—just follow these prompts, and enlist the kids' help.

TWO TO THREE WEEKS BEFORE THE PARTY

- Send invitations.
- Finalize your family's costumes.
- Decide on music and/or a playlist.
- Make decorations and test party-day crafts projects you're considering.

ONE WEEK BEFORE

- Buy nonperishable groceries and supplies.
- Prepare and organize materials for crafts projects and games.

DAY BEFORE

- Buy perishable foods.
- Prepare foods that can be made in advance.
- Assemble and fill favor bags or buckets.
- Prepare designated crafts table/area.
- Decorate.

PARTY DAY

- Prepare last-minute foods and snacks.
- Set up food and activities.
- Get into your costume, start the music, and enjoy!

decorations

Cast a spell on your home with handmade decorations that set a playful party mood. Set aside a weekend afternoon to craft a few goodies, and have the kids lend a hand. Some of the decorations are so easy you may decide to use them as a crafting activity at the party.

gauzy-glow mummy
Let this mummy pumpkin be your party beacon, *above.* When nighttime falls or you close the curtains for scary stories, it comes to life with a glow-in-the-dark coating applied to the cheesecloth strips. With its watchful eyes, the mummy is a standout in the daytime, too. See *page 113* for instructions.

dare to enter!
Make a spirited first impression by turning a sidelight window into a message board bearing a cautionary note, *this photo.* Use black and white paper and green stickers or beads for cat eyes. For the message, print large letters from a computer or trace them on black paper and cut out. Tape the letters and eyes to the glass. For a longer-lasting display, adhere inside the house.

Create tactile fun by hanging faux spider webbing and crepe paper streamers around the party room.

eye spy

Ever get that creepy feeling someone (or something) is watching you? With this feathery wreath, *above*, something is! Spread crafts glue on a 12-inch half round foam wreath. Wind a black boa or other feathery trim around the wreath, securing with pins as needed. Lay a bath towel over the wreath to gently press the feathers into the glue as it dries. For eyeballs, cut 1½- and 1-inch foam balls in half. Hot-glue googly eyes to the rounded side of each ball. Glue a 3-inch piece of wire into each cut side. Insert wire into the wreath to attach eyeballs in pairs.

long-legged spider

This friendly arachnid, *above*, is all legs—and foam balls, googly eyes, and felt scraps. The spider makes an impressive low-cost centerpiece for a buffet table or a fun crafts project for older kids. See *page 112* for instructions.

Some of the decorations you make can double as game prizes or thank-yous for adult helpers.

candy corn centerpiece

Jack-o'-lanterns, step aside! The painted dude, *above*, is a cute twist on the carved version and will last much longer.

Paint a small crafts pumpkin to mimic a piece of candy corn. Form the nose from air-drying modeling compound, such as Model Magic, and glue it to the center section. Glue googly eyes in place; draw a mouth with a black paint pen.

For shoes, cut a plastic-foam egg in half lengthwise. Paint two 12-inch-long, ½-inch-diameter dowels for the legs. Roll two 2-inch balls of modeling compound for the socks. Push one end of a dowel through each sock and then through the small end of a plastic-foam shoe. Remove the dowels. Paint the socks and shoes; let dry. Reassemble and glue the pieces to the legs. Trace around the shoes on purple and lime crafts foam for soles; glue in place.

For arms, twist together three chenille stems. Use modeling compound to form mitts on the arms. Paint the mitts to match the legs.

Cut holes or use a screwdriver to punch holes into the pumpkin for the legs and arms; secure the arms and legs with glue.

food & drinks

Your guests come in costume, so why shouldn't your treats? To keep munching frightfully fun and easy, disguise foods as spooky characters and invite partygoers to dig in!

cool ghouls

Turn frosted cupcakes into silly and sinister creations by topping them with candy, cookies, and purchased icing. Use the ingredients listed below and refer to the photo, *left*, to trick out your treats.

1 **GREEN GOBLIN** Sour gummy candy rings and straws, white and green jelly beans, mini chocolate chips

2 **WITCHY WAYS** Mini candy-coated chocolates, dyed coconut, chocolate cookie, sugar cone, purchased green icing

3 **GOING BATTY** Halved chocolate wafer cookie, candy-coated chocolate piece, sprinkles, purchased green icing

4 **SO SPOOKED** White candy-coated almonds, puffed cocoa cereal

5 **ALIEN INVASION** Dark chocolate-covered almonds

6 **PEEK A BOO** Sliced marshmallow, small mint candies, candy-coated chocolate piece, sugar

7 **WHOOO'S THERE?** Oval chocolate cookie, cashew, fruit-flavor candy circles, shaved coconut, pretzel rods, mini chocolate chips

8 **UNDER WRAPS** Candy-coated chocolate pieces, purchased green and white icing

9 **GHOSTLY FIGURE** White fondant cookie-cutter cutout

i've only got eyes for you

Watch eyes pop when you pour drinks into wacky beverage cups, *right*. For each plastic cup, use a crafts knife to cut a 1-inch-diameter plastic-foam ball in half for eyeballs. Use paint markers to color the irises, pupils, and bloodshot lines. Glue the eyeballs to the cup rim, and turn the cup upside down until the glue is dry. Add the nose and mouth (and a guest's name on the back if desired) with a black paint marker.

puddin' on a scare

With chocolate faces and cookie-crumb hair, these pudding cups, *this photo,* are an expressive and impressive snack. Use melted chocolate and a small paintbrush to paint monster faces on the insides of clear plastic cups. Refrigerate to harden the chocolate. Add green food coloring to vanilla-flavor pudding. Pour into prepared cups, top with crushed chocolate sandwich cookies, and refrigerate at least one hour. An option: Paint jack-o'-lantern faces inside the cups, substitute yellow and red food coloring to turn the pudding orange, and use pretzel logs for stems.

drink up!

Presentation counts—even with the drinks you serve. Have fun getting the liquids in the spirit with these ideas.

» For a small party, use a clear decanter to give colored beverages a potionlike presence. Bright lime-color drinks add slime appeal, and cloudy-looking ones can seem like they came straight from a mad scientist's lab. (SoBe Liz Blizz, a piña-colada-flavor juice, has a ghoulish white look.)

» If you're serving a big bowl of punch, place the bowl in a decorative black cauldron and have a designated adult—dressed as a witch—do the dipping. Similarly, you can use an ice-filled cauldron as a cooler for bottled water, juice boxes, and soft drinks.

» For a party for older children, creep up ice cubes or an ice ring by adding some well-washed plastic spiders and bugs before freezing the liquid.

Keep it simple! Paper napkins and disposable plates, cups, and utensils are the kid-friendly and sensible way to serve the goodies.

coffin confection

Kids won't rest in peace until the last crumb of this coffin cake, *left,* is devoured. The coffin is purchased pound cake and has kid-friendly assembly. Crushed cookies and worm-shape fruit snacks provide the freshly dug look. Marshmallows rolled in green sugar and a sandwich cookie form the monster. See *page 113* for the recipe.

fun & games

Even though kids have a magical way of entertaining themselves, plan to fill some party time with organized events. Have a mix of activity types, such as a sit-down crafting project followed by work-off-some-energy dance time. A costume contest is always a hit. Ask adult helpers to get into character, too!

and the winner is...
Acknowledge the creative costumes in the bunch by doling out award ribbons, *above*, to the best dressed. Set up several categories, such as most creative, silliest, or scariest, and have partygoers drop their votes into a plastic pumpkin ballot box. For award ribbons, use a circle punch or decorative-edge scissors to cut a circle from black cardstock. Cut two cardstock strips for the ribbon "tails." Glue the strips to the back of the circle; trim ends with decorative-edge scissors. Glue a smaller circle cut from Halloween-theme paper or an epoxy sticker onto the cardstock circle. Decorate with computer lettering, rub-on designs, stamps, or chipboard or foam shapes. Adhere a pin to the back.

Use a small faux pumpkin for a classic game of hot potato.

put it to music

No ghosts in your house to provide chain-rattling background noises? Get the party hopping with a playlist of Halloween-appropriate tunes. Download the suggestions below from an online site, or purchase a CD of spine-chilling sounds. Use the tunes as background music, or make a dance-off part of the day's activities.

» "Ghostbusters"
» "Thriller"
» "Monster Mash"
» "Looking for Dracula"
» "Werewolves of London"
» "The Time Warp"
» "Witch Doctor"
» "The Devil Went Down to Georgia"
» "Bad Moon Rising"
» "The Addams Family Theme"

How long should the fun last? For younger kids, a couple of hours is plenty. Older kids might be able to persuade you to stretch it into a sleepover. Either way, make sure the invitation states the time parents can pick up their kids.

merry mobile

Set up a crafts table, designate an adult helper, and let the little ghouls show their artistic side. The grinning mobile, *left*, is a cinch to make and can be hung with thread when guests get it home. Wooden embroidery-hoop rings emulate pumpkin ribbing, and crafts foam forms the grinning face. Test the project before the big day to make sure it's appropriate for the age level and time allotted. See *page 113* for instructions.

goody bucket

Dole out prizes or party favors, such as bags of candy corn, from a festive bucket that doubles as a table decoration, *this photo*. Decorate a purchased paint can with scrapbooking paper and letters. Adhere a cardstock cat face (see *page 112* for patterns). Spread glue on eyes and sprinkle with mini beads (or cut eyes from double-stick adhesive for easy adhesion on both sides).

do the shutterbug!

Preserve the fun (and ideas for future costumes) by taking lots of pictures.

- » Set up a do-it-yourself photo booth on an empty wall. Hang or tape a large piece of fabric or bedsheet to the wall for the background, add a few props, and encourage guests to strike silly poses. A sign, such as "Freaky Photos This Way," will pique interest.
- » Designate a helper to roam the room snapping candids or recording video of the action.
- » Place disposable cameras on tables to let young kids capture their own fun. Granted, you'll end up with some wasted photos, but it's a fun icebreaker and activity.
- » After the party, mail a few photos to guests for their scrapbooks. Or upload digital photos to a secure photo-sharing website or social media site, and make a private album to share electronically.

Cute-as-a-Bug Party Set

MATERIALS

Paper: black and purple
Scissors: straight and decorative edge
Circle stencil
Stencil brush
Apple Barrel acrylic paint: Kiwi 20221, White 20503, Black 20504, Pewter Grey 20580, Concord Grape 20595
Four 1-inch googly eyes
Liner paintbrush
Glue stick
Adhesive-foam dots
White paper bag
Cardstock: black and white
Black chenille stems
Hot-glue gun and glue sticks
Miscellaneous treats and party favors
$1\frac{1}{4}$-inch foam ball
Spider-shape plastic ring

INSTRUCTIONS

Invitation

Cut a 5×7-inch rectangle from black paper. Stencil the bug body on the black rectangle using the circle stencil, stencil brush, and Kiwi paint. Glue two googly eyes above the body. Cut a zigzag-edge partial circle in the bottom right-hand corner of the black rectangle to look like a bug took a bite. Use the liner brush and White paint to paint "Come Join Me," antennae, legs, fangs, and a squiggly border.

Use the liner brush and White paint to paint "I won't bite" on another piece of black paper. Cut around phrase, using a squiggly motion. Use a glue stick to adhere the cut paper to a slightly larger piece of purple paper.

Glue the black "Come Join Me" rectangle to an 8×6-inch purple rectangle. Use the liner brush and Black paint to paint "Oops!" on the bottom right-hand corner of the purple paper. Use adhesive foam to attach the "I won't bite" sign. Write party details on back of invitation.

Favor Bag

Use the circle stencil, stencil brush, and Concord Grape, Pewter Grey, Black, and Kiwi paints to stencil circles on the paper bag.

Cut a $2\frac{1}{2}\times4\frac{3}{4}$-inch rectangle from black paper. Use the liner brush and White paint to paint "Happy Halloween" on the rectangle. Cut a $5\frac{1}{4}\times2\frac{3}{4}$-inch rectangle from purple paper. Glue the black rectangle to the purple.

Cut a circle for the bug head from black cardstock. Paint the circle with Kiwi paint. Let dry. Cut two circles from white cardstock for eyes and two circles from black cardstock for irises. Use adhesive foam to attach irises to eyes. Cut a chenille stem in half, hot-glue to the back of the bug face; curl free ends for antennae. Outline the face and eyes in Black paint. Hot-glue the eyes to the face. Paint the mouth Black and fangs White.

Fill the bag with treats and party favors. Fold bag down and staple. Hot-glue the bug face to the top of the bag where stapled. Hot-glue the "Happy Halloween" sign toward the bottom.

Ring

Paint the foam ball with Kiwi paint. Let dry. Paint on two White triangle-shape fangs and a Black mouth. Let dry.

Push the edges of two googly eyes into the top of the foam ball to make indentions. Hot-glue the eyes in place. Hot-glue cut chenille stems in place for antennae. Hot-glue the bug to the top of the plastic ring.

Long-Legged Spider

MATERIALS

Foam balls: four $1\frac{1}{2}$ inch, one $2\frac{1}{2}$ inch
Eight 16-inch-long pieces of wire
Black acrylic crafts paint
Paintbrush
Hot-glue gun and glue sticks
$\frac{3}{8}$-inch googly eyes
Crafts glue
Scrap of orange felt

Goody Bucket
CAT
Enlarge 200%.
Note: Go to BHG.com/HTTbookCat to print the pattern from your computer.

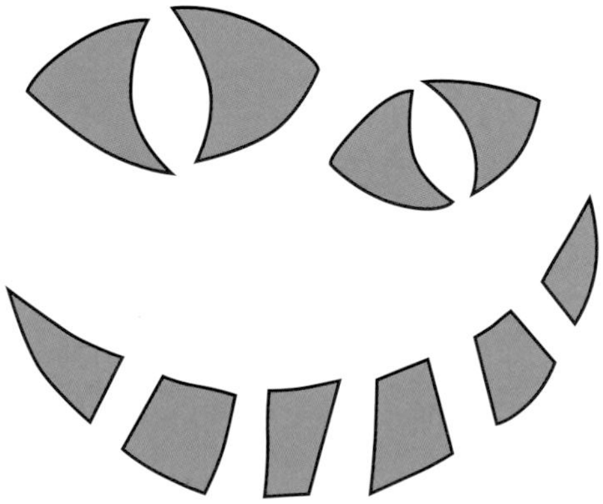

INSTRUCTIONS

Cut the 1½-inch foam balls in half with a knife. Paint the foam ball, half balls, and wires black. Bend the wires about 4 inches from the end to form knees. Hot-glue shorter ends into the sides of the 2½-inch foam ball, four to a side. Glue a half ball to the other end of each wire, making sure the ball sits flat on the tabletop. Attach googly eyes to the spider body with crafts glue. Cut eyebrows and mouth from felt; glue onto spider face.

Gauzy-Glow Mummy

MATERIALS

Cheesecloth
Fabric stiffener
Faux pumpkin
Hot-glue gun and glue sticks
1-inch googly eyes
Crafts knife
Black acrylic paint
Paintbrush
Glow-in-the-dark gel paint (We used Plaid Glo Away.)

INSTRUCTIONS

Cut cheesecloth into 4×12-inch strips. Fold in half lengthwise. Apply fabric stiffener, following manufacturer's instructions. Apply strips to the pumpkin, leaving top and bottom uncovered. Let dry.

Hot-glue googly eyes to the pumpkin. Cut four 4×6-inch strips of cheesecloth. Fold in half lengthwise. Apply fabric stiffener, following manufacturer's instructions. Cover top and bottom of each eye in a diagonal so a little of the eyes peek out. Let dry.

Use the crafts knife to cut a small mouth. Paint the inside of the mouth with the black acrylic paint. Brush glow-in-the-dark gel paint onto the cheesecloth.

Coffin Confection

INGREDIENTS

⅓ cup grape-flavor sugar-sweetened soft drink mix
2 tablespoons hot water
4 ounces cream cheese, softened
1 cup frozen whipped topping, thawed
4 chocolate sandwich cookies
1 10¾-ounce frozen pound cake, thawed
10 miniature marshmallows
1 large marshmallow
1 tablespoon green sugar
Black decorating gel
3 worm-shape chewy fruit snacks

INSTRUCTIONS

Place drink mix in a large bowl. Add hot water. Stir until mix is dissolved. Add cream cheese. Beat with electric mixer on medium speed until blended. Gently stir in whipped topping with wire whisk. Reserve ½ teaspoon of the cream cheese mixture.

Crush three cookies; place crumbs in shallow flat dish. Cut cake lengthwise in half; place in the crumb-lined dish. Frost cake bottom with some of the cream cheese mixture. Place cake top next to cake bottom to resemble a coffin lid. Frost all sides with cream cheese mixture. Sprinkle cookie crumbs along edge of lid.

Dip marshmallows in water; shake gently to remove excess water. Roll in colored sugar until evenly coated.

Place remaining cookie in center of cake bottom to resemble a body. Line up two rows of three miniature marshmallows at bottom of body for legs. Place two miniature marshmallows on sides of body for arms. Place large marshmallow at top of body for head. Using reserved cream cheese mixture, attach two miniature marshmallows to sides of head for ears. Use decorating gel to draw a mouth and eyes. Decorate with worm-shape fruit snacks.

Merry Mobile

MATERIALS

Wooden embroidery hoops
Orange brush-on glitter paint
Foam brush
Black crafts foam
Clear polyester thread
Thin sewing needle
Tacky glue

INSTRUCTIONS

Paint the hoops with glitter paint. Draw a mouth, nose, and eyes on paper to make a template. Use scissors and paper templates to cut features from black crafts foam. With the needle and thread, poke a hole through the top of each face piece; tie to the inner ring.

Glue the outer ring at a right angle to the inner ring. Tie a piece of thread to the hoop screw to hang.

Sweet Skeleton
TREAT BAG
Enlarge 200%.
Note: Go to BHG.com/HTTbookSkeleton to print the pattern from your computer.

Jack-o'-Lantern
TREAT TOPPER
Full Size Pattern
Note: Go to BHG.com/HTTbookTopper to print the pattern from your computer.

NERDS

costumes

Spark imaginations. Whether it's a wild animal, a favorite fantasy, or a grown-up career, kids' costumes are surprisingly easy to create. With clever ideas, simple techniques, and easy-to-understand instructions, making their wishes real is no dream.

wild THINGS

Help your little one transform into a cute-as-can-be creature by using our easy-to-follow instructions and patterns.

WRITTEN BY **HEIDI PALKOVIC**

octo-baby

This sea creature is swimming in cuteness—especially for the baby who has just learned to sit up. Turn kids' tights or knee-high socks into octopus tentacles with the help of stuffing and felt furniture pads for suction cups. You only need to make six. Baby's legs peek out from among the stuffed ones to complete the octo-arrangement.

mice are nice

Forget shrieks of fright. These cute mice are sure to elicit squeals of delight. Turn a basic gray hoodie into a scurry-ready ensemble with the addition of a soft chenille tummy and perky velveteen ears and tail. Finish the costume with cool sunglasses for "eyes," and attach a whiskered felt nose.

feathered friend

Who's that peeking out of her nest? This freshly hatched baby bird is ready to fledge this Halloween. Feather boas and a purchased twig wreath embellished with artificial leaves and scraps of kraft paper help this costume take flight in no time.

time to chill

This dapper dude is as cool as ice in a black sweat suit turned playful penguin getup. Create the wings, the tails, and the tummy using felt. Top off the costume with a fleece winter hat embellished with felt facial features. Add a fun finishing touch with a big catch of foam-core fish and a dowel fishing pole.

Octo-Baby

MATERIALS

Three pairs of kids' tights or adult knee-high socks
Polyester fiberfill
Hot-glue gun and glue sticks
Felt furniture pads
Wide ribbon
Adhesive-backed hook-and-loop tape
Onesie with matching hat

INSTRUCTIONS

Cut the legs off the tights and stuff each leg with polyester fiberfill. Fold the cut edges to the inside, and hot-glue the opening closed. Hot-glue felt furniture pads onto one side of each octopus "arm."

To create a belt, cut a length of ribbon that will fit around the child's waist, and glue the sealed end of each octopus arm to the ribbon, spacing so the arms fill the belt. Attach adhesive-backed hook-and-loop tape to the ends of the ribbon belt to use as a closure. Dress the child in a onesie and hat. Secure the ribbon belt around the child's waist.

DESIGNED BY **CATHERINE RYAN**
PHOTOGRAPHY BY **JENNY RISHER**

Baby Bird

MATERIALS

Light blue long-sleeve onesie with hood
Feather boas: orange and light blue
Fabric glue
Yellow felt
Grapevine wreath (large enough to fit comfortably around child's waist)
Hot-glue gun and glue sticks
Artificial leaves
Kraft paper
Wide ribbon
Orange tights
Yellow shoes

INSTRUCTIONS

Create the baby bird's tummy by adhering the orange feather boa to the front of the light blue onesie using fabric glue.

Cut a 6-inch-square beak from yellow felt. Fold diagonally and glue the folded edge to the top edge of the hood. Glue a light blue feather boa around the hood edge without covering the beak. Glue two light blue feather boa pieces around the sleeves at the wrists. Let dry.

Hot-glue artificial leaves and strips of kraft paper to the grapevine wreath. Cut two long lengths from ribbon to create shoulder straps (you'll want to measure the length needed on your child). Tie each ribbon to the wreath, positioning and adjusting the length to fit over the child's shoulders. Add orange tights and yellow shoes to complete the look.

DESIGNED BY **CARRIE NAUMANN**
PHOTOGRAPHY BY **ADAM ALBRIGHT**

Mouse

MATERIALS

Gray zip-front hooded sweatshirt
½ yard of white or pink minky dot chenille
Sewing machine
Fabric glue
Adhesive-backed hook-and-loop tape
1 yard of gray velveteen
Polyester fiberfill
Felt: pink and white
¾ yard of black cord
Sunglasses
Black pom-pom
Pink ribbon (for girl mouse)

INSTRUCTIONS

Note: Three sizes for the tummy pattern are provided in the pattern section, opposite. Choose the one closest to the sweatshirt size you're using. Enlarge each pattern piece as indicated.

Using the appropriate tummy pattern, cut the pieces from white or pink dot chenille. Turn all edges under ⅛ inch, and either machine-sew or use fabric glue to hold the edges in place. Using a narrow zigzag stitch, sew the outside edges of the tummy pieces to the front of the sweatshirt. Overlap the right front piece over the zipper, and stitch along the zipper edge to form a flap to cover the zipper. Adhere self-adhesive hook-and-loop tape inside the flap to attach to the other tummy piece.

Using the ear patterns, cut four outer ear pieces from velveteen and two inner ear pieces from white or pink dot chenille. Stitch or glue one pink or white inner ear to the center of one gray outer ear piece. With right sides together, sew one outer ear piece with an inner ear embellishment and one plain gray ear piece together, leaving a ½-inch opening. Turn right side out through the opening. Repeat to make a second ear. Referring to the photo, *right*, for placement, hand-sew the ears to the top of the sweatshirt hood.

Using the pattern, cut the tail from gray velveteen. With right sides together, sew the long edges of the tail together. Turn right side out and stuff with fiberfill. Hand-sew the tail to the lower back of the sweatshirt, *left*.

Using the nose patterns, cut the pieces from pink felt. Cut the teeth from white felt using the patterns. With right sides together, sew the nose pieces together to make a cone. Cut six 3½-inch lengths from black cord, knot one end of each piece, then use a needle to thread the pieces through the nose as indicated by the circles on the top nose pattern. Glue teeth to bottom of the nose as indicated on the pattern. Wrap the felt tab around the bridge of the sunglasses, and glue or hand-sew it in place. Glue a pom-pom to the end of nose.

For a girly mouse, cut a 2½×30-inch length from gray velveteen for the ruffle around the hood. Fold the piece in half lengthwise with right sides together; use a gathering foot on your sewing machine to create a ruffle. If you don't have a gathering foot, use fabric glue to hold gathers in place. Sew or glue the ruffle to the inside edge of the hood, trimming the excess at the ends if necessary. Tie short lengths of pink ribbon in bows around the ears and the tail.

DESIGNED BY **CARRIE NAUMANN**
PHOTOGRAPHY BY **ADAM ALBRIGHT**

Mouse Costume

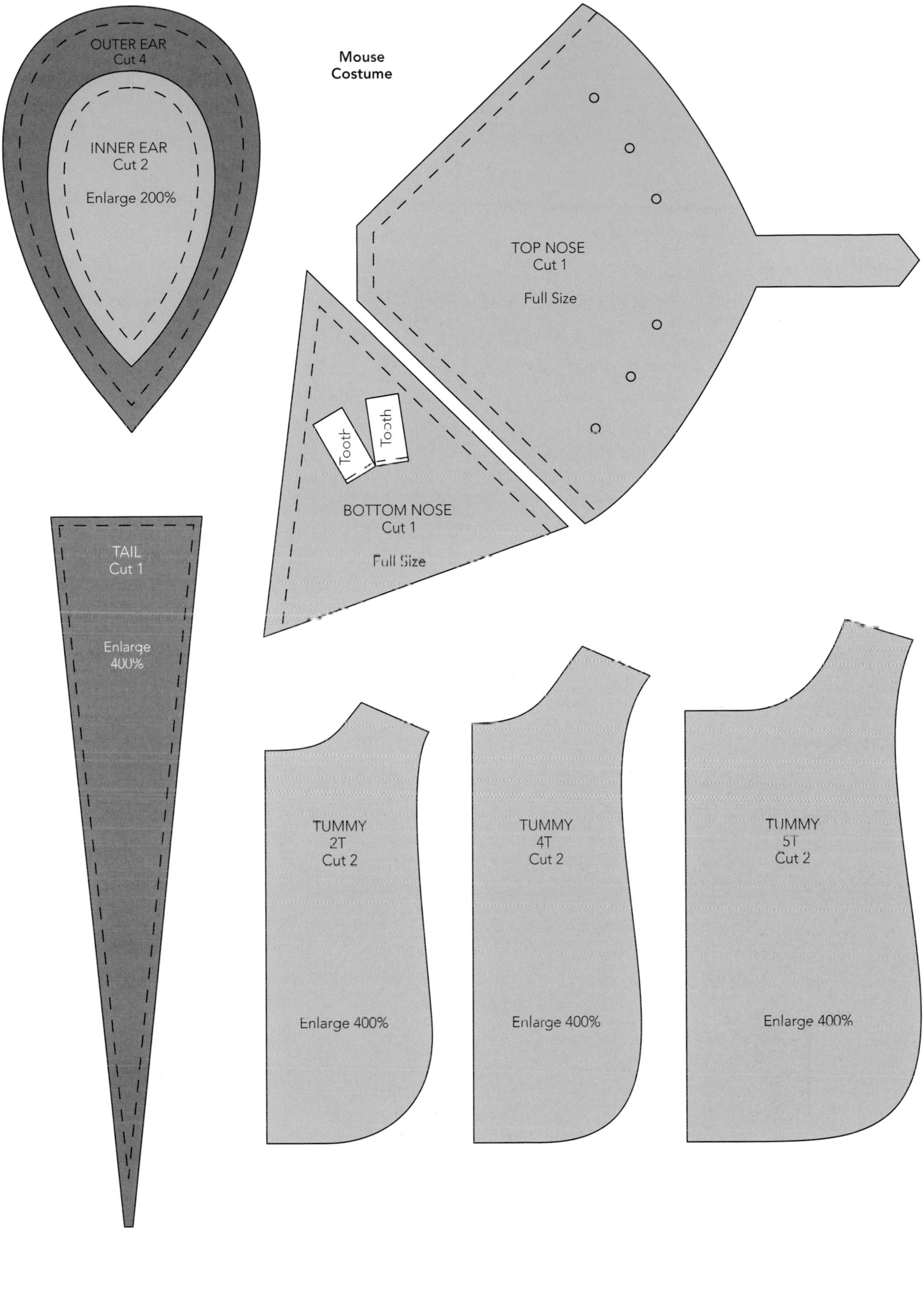

Penguin

MATERIALS

¾ yard of white felt
Scallop-edge scissors
Black sweatshirt
Fabric glue
1 yard of black felt
Green polka-dot ribbon
Three black buttons
Black fleece hat with chin strap
Scraps of gray, yellow, and pink felt
White foam-core board
Crafts knife
Markers
1-inch-thick plastic-foam sheet
White cord
Fishing bobber
Dowel

INSTRUCTIONS

Note: Enlarge the patterns, opposite, as indicated or adjust to fit your child.

Cut the penguin shirt from white felt using the pattern. Cut six ½×16-inch strips from white felt, trimming one long edge of each with scallop-edge scissors. Cut one 1½×16-inch strip from white felt.

Lay out the scalloped strips and the 1½×16-inch strip on the front of the shirt piece as shown in the photograph, *left,* and glue or topstitch the pieces in place. Trim the ends of the strips as needed. Glue or topstitch the embellished shirt to the front of the sweatshirt.

Using the patterns, cut the collar pieces from white felt and the arm and tail pieces from black felt.

Glue or sew the collar pieces to the neckline of the sweatshirt, each arm piece to a shoulder seam of the sleeves, and the tail pieces to the bottom back of the sweatshirt.

Glue or sew each arm to the cuff of the sweatshirt, allowing the point to extend over the hand but leaving plenty of room for movement.

Create a bow tie from the ribbon, and glue it just below the neckline. Sew three buttons to the center of the shirt.

For the penguin head, cut out the eye pieces from white, gray, and black felt as shown on the patterns. Cut out the beak from yellow felt and the cheeks from pink felt. Glue or sew the pieces to the hat as shown in the photograph, *above*, layering the eyes first and then the beak on top of the eyes. Finish by gluing or sewing the cheeks in place.

Using the fish patterns as templates, trace the fish onto white foam-core board and cut out with a crafts knife. Transfer the details with black marker. Color the fish with markers.

Cut 1-inch cubes from plastic foam using a crafts knife. Pierce a small hole through the top and bottom of the fish and string each fish on a length of white cord along with plastic-foam cubes. String one fish and a plastic fishing bobber onto a length of cord; tie the other end to a wooden dowel to make a fishing pole.

DESIGNED BY **CARRIE NAUMANN**
PHOTOGRAPHY BY **ADAM ALBRIGHT**

Penguin
Enlarge all Fish pattern pieces 200%.
Enlarge remaining pattern pieces 250%.

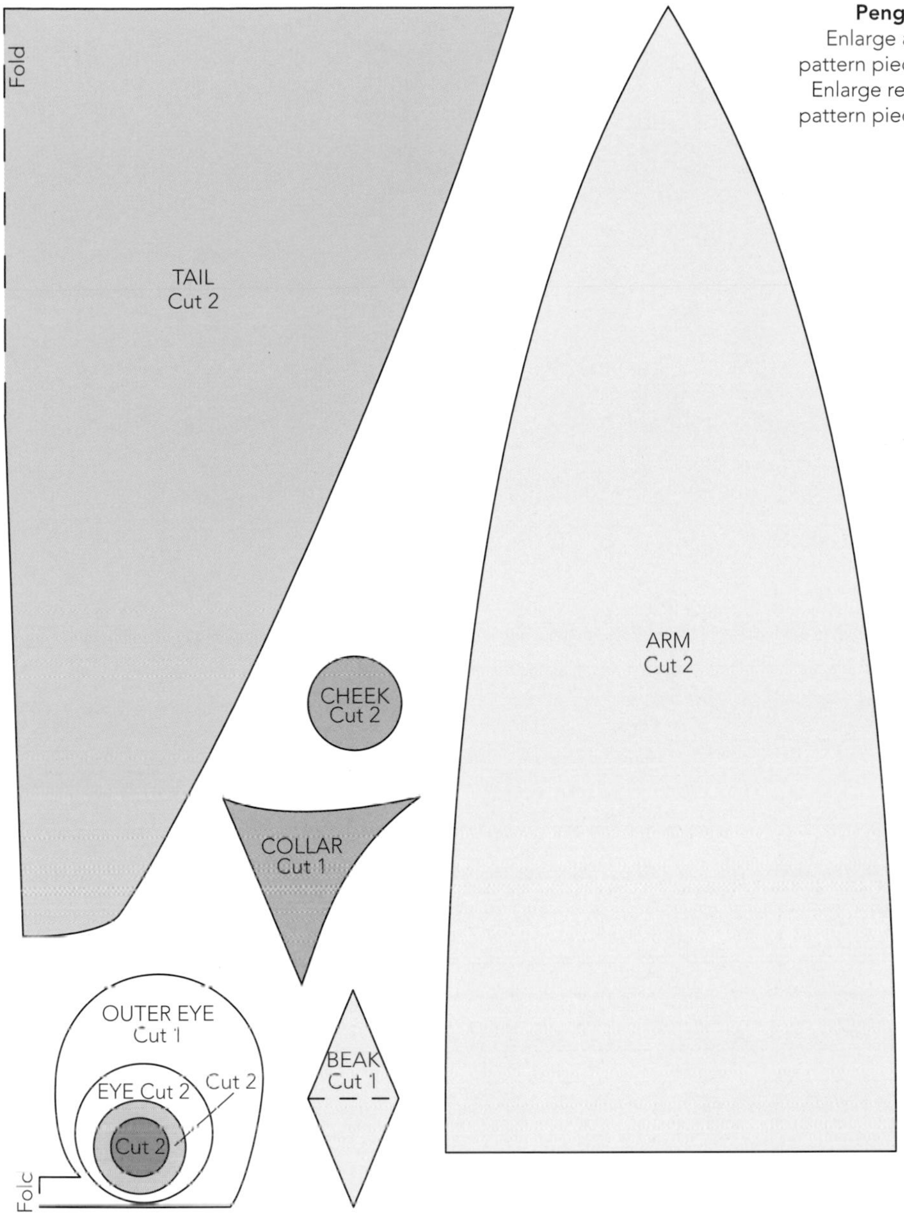

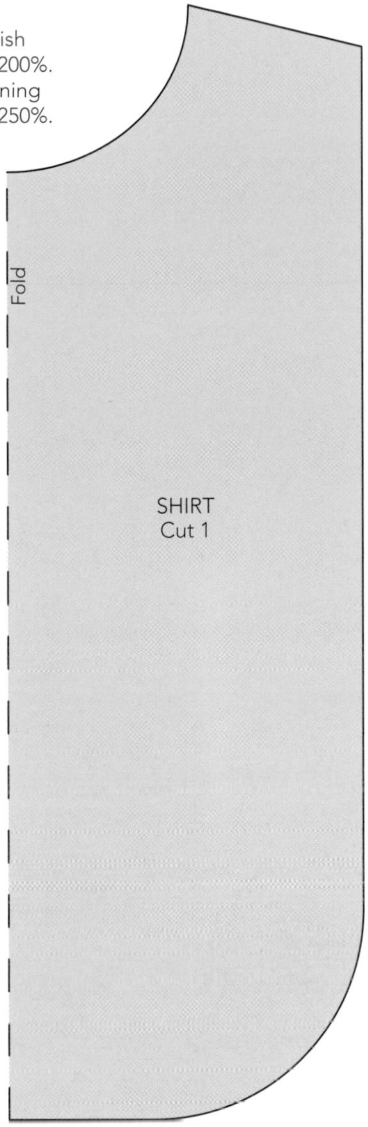

WHEN I grow up

Ask kids what they want to be someday, and you're certain to hear lofty plans. Using our instructions, these easy-to-make Halloween costumes help them fulfill their dreams.

DESIGNED BY **HEIDI BOYD** WRITTEN BY **HEIDI PALKOVIC**
PHOTOGRAPHY BY **JAY WILDE**

rembrandt in training
Your busy little guys or gals may be into finger-paint creations, but that doesn't mean they can't play the part of a renowned artist this Halloween. The key to this pièce de résistance is an artist's smock created by dripping and splattering colorful paint onto an oversize shirt. Just slip on the smock, add a beret, and complete the artsy look with a paintbrush.

sweet-as-can-be cupcake chef

Sugar and spice and everything nice—that's what this costume is made of. To create this sweet costume, stamp hearts on a child's apron and chef's hat with acrylic paint, and pipe on details with puff paint. Sweeten the look with ruffle trim glued or stitched to the apron and hatband. Then whip up a batch of tulle cupcakes decorated with crafts-foam frosting, and serve them on a foil platter.

take-a-bow ballerina

This recital-inspired ballerina ensemble begins with a leotard, tutu, headband, and tights—all you have to do is embellish with beads and pearls, silk flowers, and tulle. Give your ballerina a realistic "en pointe" touch by dressing up sparkly flats with long ribbons for crisscrossing laces. To punch up the twirly effect, make wristbands using elastic and ribbons, and then watch your little one command a repeat performance!

ready to rock

Forget auditions and touring—your little guitar hero will be ready for a showstopping performance at any Halloween gig in this costume. Turn basic jeans and a plain white T-shirt into a stage-ready wardrobe with iron-on additions that include a rhinestone skull and crossbones, metal studs, and colorful block lettering. Attach a custom-made studded cover to a toy guitar strap, and let the jamming begin!

fairy-tale favorite

If your little one's dreams focus on happily ever after instead of careers or stardom, this beloved character of fairy-tale fame might be just right for this year's costume. Little Red Riding Hood jumps off the page and into real life with the help of a hooded red cape made from red felt and black trim. A stuffed-toy wolf nestled into a napkin-lined basket adds to the fun.

Artist

MATERIALS

White button-front large shirt
Acrylic paints in several colors
Toothbrush
Regular paintbrush
White plastic painter's palette (optional)
Large artist's brush (optional)
Beret

INSTRUCTIONS

Cut off the shirtsleeves at the desired length. Stuff the shirt with crumpled paper, and lay it on a protected work surface. Using the toothbrush, paintbrush, and different-color paints, randomly drip and spatter paint over the shirt. To make a colorful accessory for your artist to carry, squeeze a different paint color into each section of the palette. Let the palette dry thoroughly. Use the beret, palette, and artist's brush to complete the costume.

Rock Star

MATERIALS

Dark or black jeans
Iron-on rhinestone skull-and-crossbones patch
Iron-on silver square studs (available in strips)
White T-shirt
Iron-on black and red block letters
Fabric glue
¼ yard of skull-and-crossbones printed fabric
Adhesive hook-and-loop tape
Toy guitar with strap

INSTRUCTIONS

Following the manufacturer's instructions, apply the skull-and-crossbones patch to a pant leg and a strip of studs to each pant leg; apply the block letters to the T-shirt to spell "ROCK" or the desired word.

On the right side of the skull-and-crossbones fabric, apply a strip of iron-on studs lengthwise about 3 inches from one long edge of the fabric. Lay the embellished strip stud-side down. Fold the fabric, wrong sides together, so the stud strip is about ½ inch from one folded fabric edge; fold the raw edges under slightly and overlap edges. Press folds. Adhere the fabric edges with fabric glue.

Place the skull-and-crossbones cover over a toy guitar's strap, securing it with strips of hook-and-loop tape.

Cupcake Chef

MATERIALS

Pink youth apron and chef's hat
Acrylic paint: white and pink
Artist's brush
Heart-shape crafts-foam stamps
Puff paint: white and pink
1¼ yards of white ruffle trim
Fabric glue
Silver foil tray
Large round paper doily
Hot-glue gun and glue sticks
Five white chenille stems
Silver foil cupcake liners
⅓ yard of fuchsia tulle
Crafts-foam sheet: white
Crafts-foam stickers: hearts and flowers
Five sparkly pom-poms

INSTRUCTIONS

With pink acrylic paint and an artist's brush, paint the outline of a large heart on the apron bib and each pocket. Or brush pink paint onto a large heart stamp; press hearts onto apron; let dry.

Brush white acrylic paint onto a small heart stamp, and press several hearts inside the large pink hearts. If stamping large hearts, outline large hearts with pink puff paint. Clean small heart stamp; brush it with pink acrylic paint and press into the center of each large heart.

Cut lengths of white ruffle trim to fit bib and pocket edges. Attach trim to apron with fabric glue.

Brush pink paint onto small heart stamp, and press hearts evenly around the hatband. Outline stamped hearts with pink puff paint. Use white puff paint to create dotted hearts between the stamped hearts.

Hot-glue the doily to the tray. Poke a hole in the center of the tray. Insert a chenille stem, extending 1 inch of the stem through the back of the tray. Twist the short end into a spiral, and secure it to the back of the tray with hot glue. Poke four more holes around the tray; insert and hot-glue chenille stems.

Poke a hole in the center of five foil cupcake liners, and slide each liner onto a chenille stem. Cut five 10-inch squares from tulle. Tie a piece around each chenille stem, tucking it into the cupcake liners.

Use the patterns, *below*, to cut five cupcake tops from crafts foam. Poke a hole in the center of each and slide onto a chenille stem. Trim the chenille stems, and fold the end over on each cupcake top.

Referring to the patterns, "frost" the tops with heart- and flower-shape foam stickers and pink and white puff paint. Hot-glue a pom-pom to the top of each cupcake.

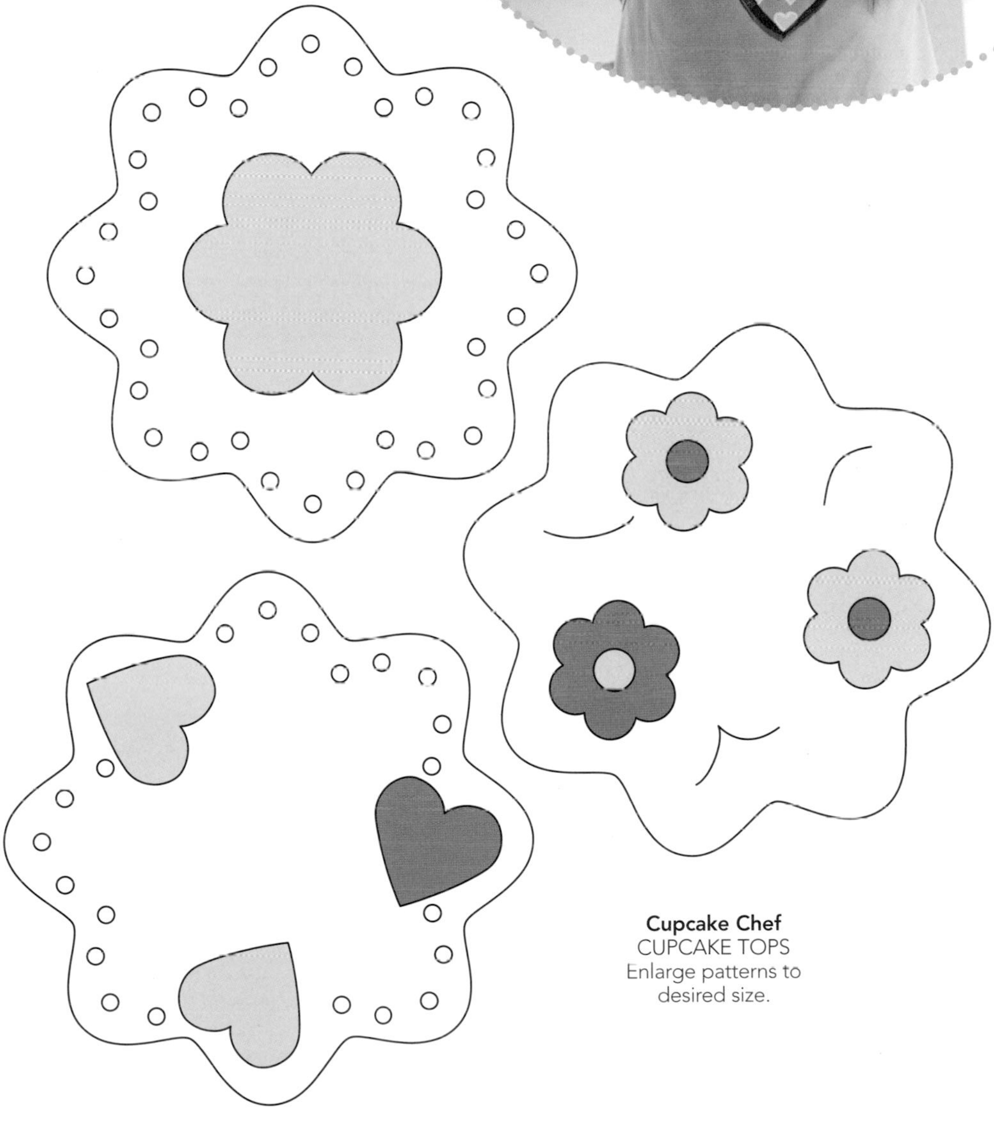

Cupcake Chef
CUPCAKE TOPS
Enlarge patterns to desired size.

Ballerina

MATERIALS

Lavender leotard
Silk flowers (pulled from silk flower stems)
Small round pearl beads
⅛ yard of lavender tulle
Satin-covered plain headband
Five large lavender pearl beads
24-gauge crafts wire
Assorted iridescent clear plastic beads
Hot-glue gun and glue sticks
Clear rhinestones
Lingerie elastic
Assorted ⅛- to ½-inch-wide silk ribbons: lavender, white, and purple
2⅔ yards of ½-inch-wide lavender silk ribbon
Sparkly flats
Tutu

INSTRUCTIONS

Use needle and thread to hand-stitch nine silk flowers and nine pearl-bead centers to the neckline of the leotard.

Fold the tulle to fit the center of the headband; arrange it over the top. String five large pearl beads onto a 12-inch length of wire. Wrap one end of the wire around one end of the headband, catching folded tulle inside the wire wrap. Continue wrapping, securing the rest of the tulle in place and positioning a single bead on the band with each wrap. Twist the end of the wire to the opposite end of the headband.

Cut a 16-inch length of wire, and wrap one end around the side of the first pearl. String a sequence of nine iridescent beads onto the wire. Pass the wire under the next pearl; continue with nine more beads, passing the wire under the next wrapped pearl each time. Wrap the wire end around one side of the last wired pearl. Shape the nine-bead sections into points to make a tiara. Hot-glue silk flowers to the headband edge to cover the wire wraps. Hot-glue rhinestones to the flower centers.

Wrap the elastic around your child's wrist, and cut it at a comfortable length. Cut five ribbons 1½ to 2 feet long. Hand-stitch the elastic ends together to form a loop. Sew the ribbons together, adding a silk flower and bead before pushing the needle through the flower to secure all the pieces to the elastic. Repeat for the second wristband.

For the slippers, cut two 4-foot long pieces from the wide silk ribbon. Hot-glue the center of one ribbon inside each slipper, leaving ends loose.

Little Red Riding Hood

MATERIALS

Sewing machine
1 yard of red felt
3 yards of black flower trim
Red grosgrain ribbon
Hot-glue gun and glue sticks
Two black pom-poms
Lace trim
Basket
Dish towel or cloth napkin
Stuffed-toy wolf

INSTRUCTIONS

Enlarge the pattern, *opposite*, to fit your child.

Fold the felt in half to cut two pattern pieces. Using the enlarged pattern, cut out the cape. Pin the cape pieces right sides together, and sew the layers along the dashed lines shown on the pattern. Turn right side out.

Stitch the flower trim to the outside edges of the cape and to the inside edge of the hood. Stitch a length of ribbon to each side of the hood for ties. Hot-glue a pom-pom to each end.

For the basket, cut the lace trim to fit around the basket edge, and hot-glue it in place. Line the basket with a dish towel or cloth napkin, and place a cuddly toy wolf inside.

Little Red Riding Hood
CAPE
Cut 2
Enlarge pattern to
desired size.

give your tail a swish

In a sea of costumes, this one makes a splash! Its satiny tail of reversible blue-and-lime quilted fabric is stitched as a skirt, with the front cut short for walking ease and the back cut long with tail fins. Just make sure your little mermaid dons leggings and a flesh-tone shirt underneath her bikini top for cool-weather trick-or-treating. Her crown is a headband decorated in yarn loops and ocean treasures.

Crafting costumes is quick when you use this simple trick: Pair basics from your child's closet with no-sew and easy-sew accessories. In less time than it takes to cast a spell, you'll conjure up magical personalities using our instructions and everything from cardboard and candy bars to felt and feather boas.

all decked out

DESIGNED BY **HEIDI BOYD**
PHOTOGRAPHY BY **JAY WILDE**

ahoy, pirate!
This pirate's got bling—and it won't cost you a chest of treasure. With inexpensive felt, gold and rickrack trims, and a bit of sewing, your little captain will be set to sail into uncharted candy territory. Provide swagger with supersize accessories: a skull-and-crossbones cap and a belt with a giant cardboard buckle wrapped in foil tape.

If costume shops bore you and elaborate patterns scare you, try these clever creations.

a sleek candy-collecting machine
Half the fun of this automaton is gathering the materials: a box, duct tape, and bike helmet from the garage; foam beads and a Slinky from the toy bin; flexible dryer duct and pipe insulation from the hardware store. Ready to compute? Just cut, spray-paint, and tape away! A treat-filled window in front leaves no doubt about this robot's mission.

what flair, princess fair!
Want to go green for Halloween? Not toad green! This regal ensemble reuses that special-occasion dress your daughter will soon outgrow and transforms it into a costume fit for a princess. Simply tie a full-length overskirt around the waist of the dress. For a hat she'll adore, fashion a mile-high cone with a veil to swirl and twirl the night away.

flitter by, butterfly
Turn a pajama cocoon into a dazzling butterfly with fabric wings so shimmery you won't need trim to make them sparkle. Just cut the wings out in one piece and add elastic and ribbon for shaping and fastening. To make your little one as fabulous as the attire, include boa-embellished headband antennae and glittery shadow and adhesive diamonds around the eyes.

Little Mermaid

MATERIALS

Sewing machine
1¼ yards of 45-inch-wide blue-and-lime reversible quilted satin
Polyester fiberfill
¼ yard of lime ruched satin fabric
½-inch-wide elastic
¾ yard of ¼-inch-wide iridescent ribbon
Silk flowers (remove stems and centers)
Plastic pearl beads: 2 white and 1 teal
1⅓ yards of ¾-inch-wide sheer white ribbon
Satin headband
Ribbon yarn: blue and lime
Darning needle
Iridescent plastic beads
Hot-glue gun and glue sticks
Seashells
E6000 adhesive

INSTRUCTIONS

For the tail, fold the quilted fabric in half. Place leggings that fit your child on top and draw the back onto the fabric, referring to the diagram, *below*. Cut out two backs. With a blue and a lime side facing, stitch the pieces together, leaving the top open. Turn right side out. Stuff the end of the tail with fiberfill and sew across the top to contain the stuffing. Make the front as directed for the back, following the front diagram. Stack the front over the back and blindstitch along the sides. Stay-stitch around the waistline.

For the waistband, cut an 8×24-inch strip of ruched fabric. With right sides together, stitch one edge of the waistband around the top of the tail. Fold the waistband in half with wrong sides facing and baste in place with elastic in between; adjust the fit. Secure the elastic ends. Slip-stitch the waistband closed.

For the bikini top, enlarge the pattern as needed and cut two shapes from quilted fabric. Sew shapes together with right sides facing, leaving openings between the dots on the pattern. Turn right side out through the largest opening; sew the opening closed. Cut iridescent ribbon into two 13-inch lengths. Slip one end of each ribbon into the top openings for straps. Sew each opening closed, and top it with a flower and pearl. Cut the sheer white ribbon into two 24-inch lengths. Slip one end of each ribbon into the side openings and sew closed. Sew a flower and pearl to the center of the bikini top.

For the crown, use half of the blue yarn to make continuous loops from 1 foot to 3 feet long. Glue the top of each loop across the headband. Repeat with the lime yarn. Cut the remaining yarn into 2- to 4-foot lengths. Fold each length in half, and thread it onto a darning needle. Thread a silk petal and an iridescent bead onto the ends. Remove the needle, and then secure the petal and beads with an overhand knot. Hot-glue the yarn folds across the headband. Glue shells in place using the E6000 adhesive.

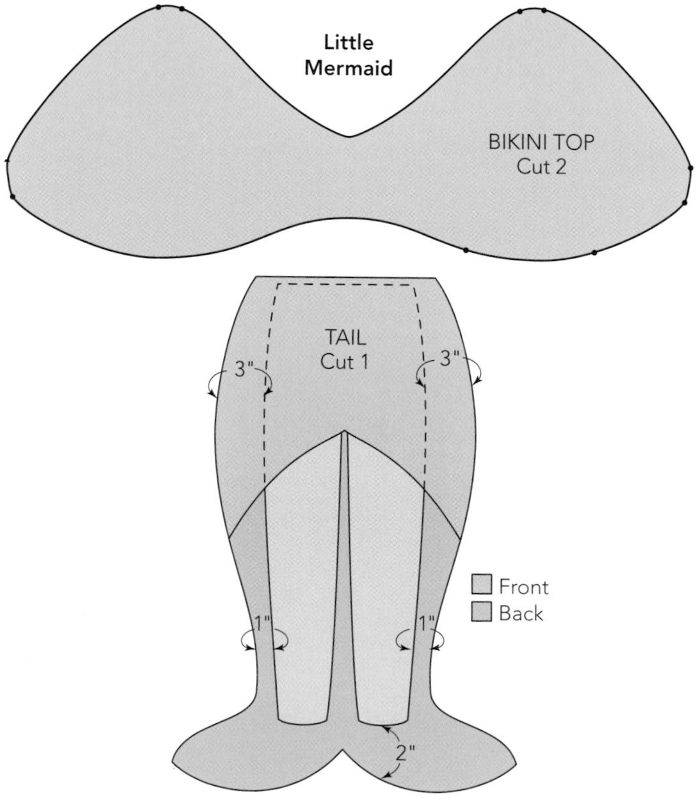

Pirate

MATERIALS

Sewing machine
¾ yard of 72-inch-wide black felt
⅝-inch-wide gold ribbon
Jumbo black-and-white rickrack
1½ yards of gold cord
Darning needle
Stiff white felt
Fabric glue
Cardboard
Foil tape
¼ yard of 54-inch-wide black faux leather

INSTRUCTIONS

For the vest, use a shirt that fits your child as a pattern. Cut a front from black felt, referring to the diagram, *below*. Cut a back, omitting the V-neck. Cut the front down the center, making two pieces. Cut two sleeve caps. Sew the front pieces to the back at the shoulders and sides. Stitch the sleeve caps in place. Topstitch gold ribbon to the edges.

For the hat, enlarge the pattern, *bottom*. Cut out two hats from black felt on the fold. Leaving pieces folded, stay-stitch ¼ inch along open edges of each shape; sew rickrack across widest point of each shape. Place with wrong sides together; sew the short sides. Overcast the top closed, using gold cord and a darning needle, sewing through outer layers only. Cut a skull and crossbones, *below right,* from white felt; glue in place. Place hat on child's head; tack at bottom edge for a snug fit.

For the belt, enlarge the buckle pattern, *bottom right,* 200 percent, and cut two from cardboard. Stack pieces and wrap in foil tape. Cut a 6×38½-inch strip of faux leather. Fold in half with right sides together and stitch, leaving an opening for turning. Turn right side out and topstitch. Wrap an end around the center bar of the buckle and sew it back onto itself.

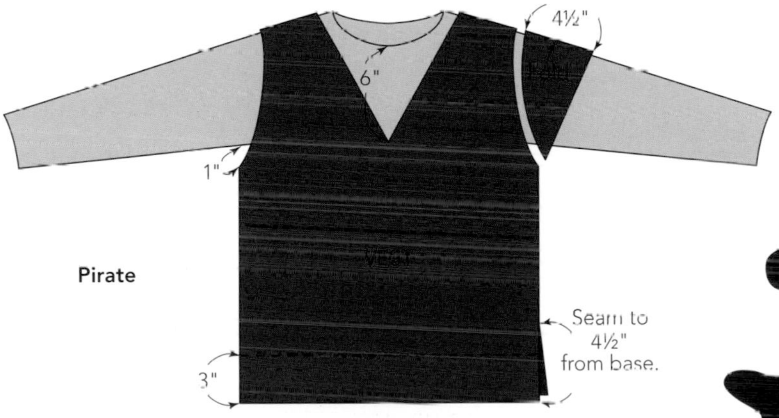

Pirate

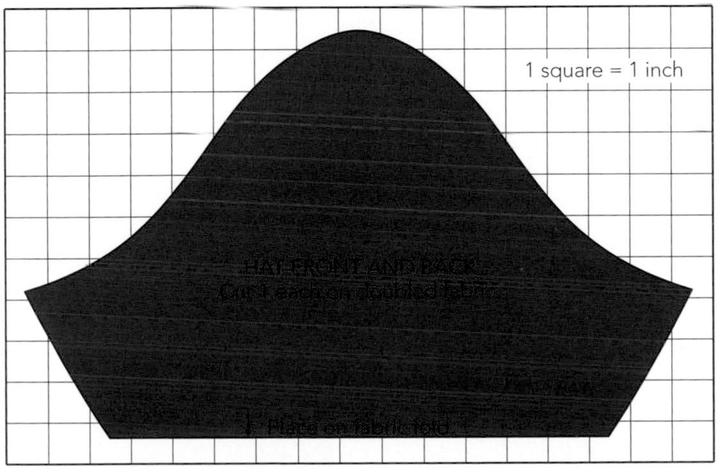

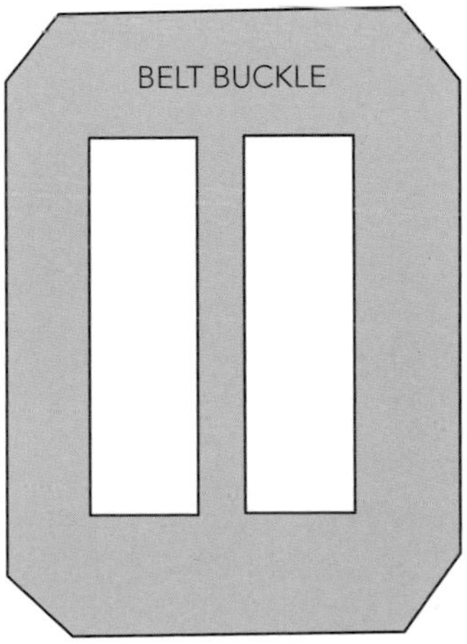

Robot

MATERIALS

Cardboard box (to fit over your child's shoulders)
10×12-inch clear poly envelope
Silver spray paint
Foil tape
⅝-inch pipe insulation
Adhesive tape
Silver mini brads
Mini wrapped candies
Assorted crafts-foam beads
Brads to fit inside foam beads
Hot-glue gun and glue sticks
Flexible dryer duct (use the clamp for the helmet)
White duct tape
Bicycle helmet
Mini Slinky toy, cut in half
E6000 adhesive

INSTRUCTIONS

Remove the bottom from the box. Cut out a circle on the top. Check the fit over your child's head. Mark the armhole locations. Remove the box and cut out the armholes. Using the poly envelope as a template, draw a rectangle on the box front. Cut out the rectangle ½ inch inside the drawn shape. Spray-paint the box silver. Cover all edges with foil tape.

Cut a slit down the length of the pipe insulation. Wrap the insulation around the head opening and the bottom half of each armhole opening.

Copy a clip-art gauge image, and tape it to the inside of the envelope. Secure it to the envelope with a brad.

Tape the poly envelope inside the box, centering it in the rectangle opening. Fill it with candies, and tape it closed. Glue beads and brads to the box front.

For arms and legs, divide the dryer duct into four equal pieces. Fold over the cut edges and cover with duct tape. Spray the helmet silver. Glue foam beads with brads to the front. Pull the dryer duct clamp apart so the wire spans the helmet top. Thread the Slinky onto the clamp. Push the Slinky and clamp ends into the foam core inside the helmet. Apply E6000 adhesive where the wires enter the foam core to stabilize.

Princess

MATERIALS

1½ yards of 54-inch-wide pink satin
Fray Check (or clear nail polish)
Sewing machine
1½-inch-wide purple wire-edge ribbon
¼ yard of quilted polyester fabric
Hot-glue gun and glue sticks
⅔ yard of ½-inch-wide sequin trim
⅔ yard of 2-inch-wide fur trim
1½ yards of pink netting
White elastic cord

INSTRUCTIONS

For the skirt, fold the satin in half. Determine the desired length of skirt and mark on fabric. Measure the child's waist; multiply by 1½ and divide by 2. Mark this measurement on the top edge of the folded fabric. Referring to the diagram, *opposite, top left*, draw scallops along hemline. Cut out skirt. Apply Fray Check to the edges. Run gathering stitches along waistline. Gather the skirt to fit. Cut purple ribbon to fit around the waist plus 36 inches. Center and sew the ribbon atop the gathers. Cut another piece of ribbon to fit the waist. Stitch to the inside of the waistband.

For the hat, enlarge the pattern, *opposite, top right*; cut one shape each from the satin and quilted fabrics. With right sides together, sew shapes together, leaving an opening for turning. Turn right side out. Sew opening closed.

Fold the hat in half, with the satin inside. Sew the straight edges together. Glue the sequin and fur trims around the bottom. Turn the hat right side out. Turn up the decorated brim.

Stitch the center of the netting to the tip of the hat, and then push the tip into the hat 1 inch. Add an elastic-cord chin strap.

Princess

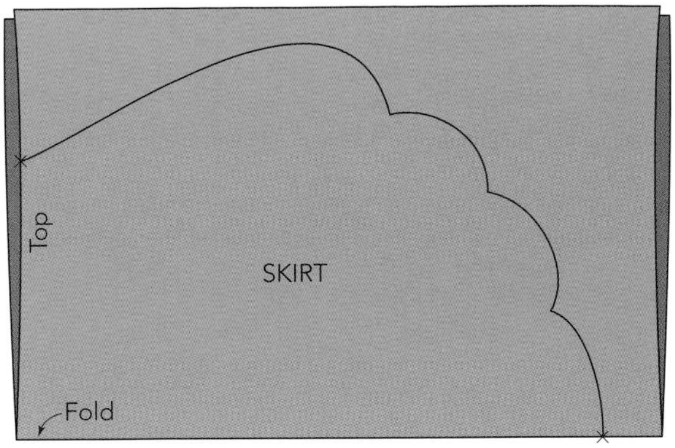

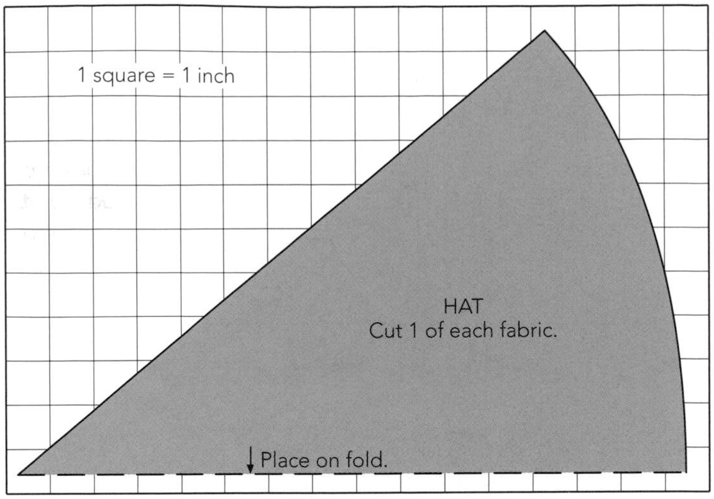

Butterfly

MATERIALS

1¼ yards of fabric
Fray Check (or clear nail polish)
2⅔ yards of ¼-inch-wide pink ribbon
Pink pom-poms: six ¾-inch and two 1¼-inch
Hot-glue gun and glue sticks
⅔ yard of elastic cord
6½ inches of ¾-inch-wide elastic
Two white chenille stems
Satin-covered headband
1 yard of ½-inch-diameter pink feather boa

INSTRUCTIONS

For the wings, use a shirt that fits your child to create the pattern. Cut the wings from fabric, referring to the diagram, *right*. Apply Fray Check to the edges.

For neck ties, cut a 32-inch length of ribbon. Stitch the center of the ribbon to the center top of the wings; glue a large pom-pom to each ribbon end.

Cut two 10-inch lengths of elastic cord. Knot the ends together for two wristbands. Stitch each wristband to the highest point on each wing.

Cut two 9-inch lengths of ribbon. Fold the ribbons in half, and glue the fold over the elastic knots. Glue a small pom-pom to each ribbon end.

For the waistband, center the wide elastic on the inside of the wings and hand-sew around the outside edge of the elastic, stretching it as you sew. Cut two 22-inch lengths of ribbon and stitch to each end of the elastic.

Adhere a small pom-pom to each ribbon end.

For the antennae, wrap one chenille stem in half around the headband. Twist the stem ends together, slipping a 2-inch piece of boa between the ends at the top. Repeat for the second antenna. Fold the rest of the boa in half, and glue it to the top of the headband.

Butterfly

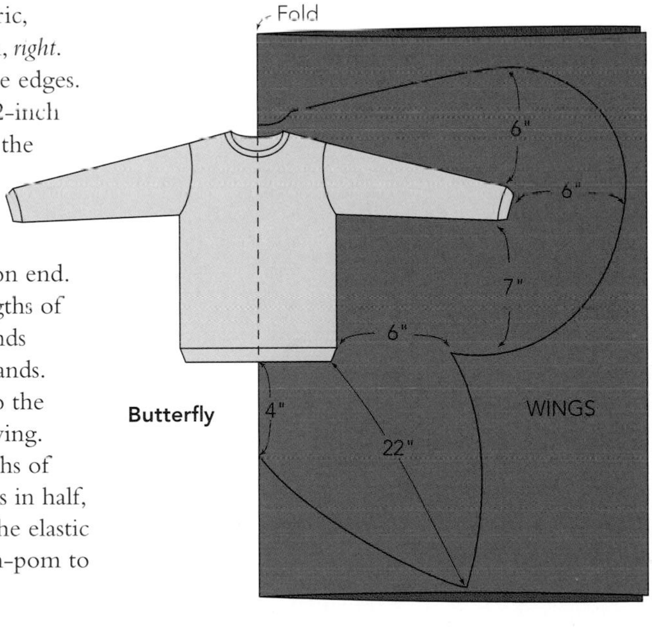

treats

They're kooky and they're spooky, but most of all they're tasty goodies. Sweet and savory foods put on party attire and become celebration stars. The haunting disguises might make guests hesitate, but one bite will never be enough to satisfy their Halloween hunger.

Every Halloween, kids and party guests arrive in costume. Now the food can dress up too. These tantalizing treats will either leave them staring . . . or have them digging in for more!

FOOD STYLED BY **DIANNA NOLIN** WRITTEN BY **LAURA HOLTORF COLLINS** PHOTOGRAPHY BY **MARTY BALDWIN**

eerie EDIBLES

night eyes

They don't call them dEVILed for nothing. Whip up a batch of your favorite picnic eggs, and turn them wild-eyed for Halloween with a few choice veggies. They're a perfect treat for kids or adults with bottomless pits to fill.

gremlins rule!
Infuse your brews with grinning kiwi gremlins kept on ice until you're ready to party. Grenadine—a sweet red syrup—makes a wicked addition to the beverage mix. Use lemonade instead of the margarita mix for a kooky kid-friendly concoction.

ghouls just wanna have fun
Pop one of these little ghouls into your mouth and you're in for a big surprise. Purchased fondant draped over single or stacked 'mallows forms a delicious disguise.

wacky witches

With a little hocus-pocus, cheesecake and cookies turn into witch hats, lime sherbet or pistachio ice cream casts a ghastly pallor for faces, and cashews and sprinkles hook up for noses. Add shredded coconut for tangled, broom-riding hair, and—poof—this duo magically appears. Eat them right away, or keep them in the freezer to prevent an early demise.

tombstone trio

These three spine-tingling skeletons lie in freshly dug graves in a lonely boneyard (the crypts are actually chocolate graham crackers atop green-tinted coconut and piles of cracker-crumb "dirt"). Sandwich cookies stand in for terrifying tombstones, and the alabaster bones are pretzel sticks dipped in melted white chocolate. Piped melted chocolate transforms sweet marshmallows into the haunting heads of these bygone boys.

jack-o'-lantern cheese balls

You'll turn cream cheese into a total goofball when you dress it up as a playful pumpkin head. Nacho cheese–flavored snack chips bring a crunchy coat of orange, while black olive pieces add that deranged smile and those haunting vacant eyes. Top with a baby dill pickle to stand in for a stem, and this silly spook is ready to relish.

spooky stew

Every party needs a few hearty offerings to balance the snacks and sweets. You can turn shepherd's pie into a ghoulish delight when you top individual servings of the meaty stew with whipped potatoes piped into ghostly shapes. Murky green capers give these specters their creepy beady eyes.

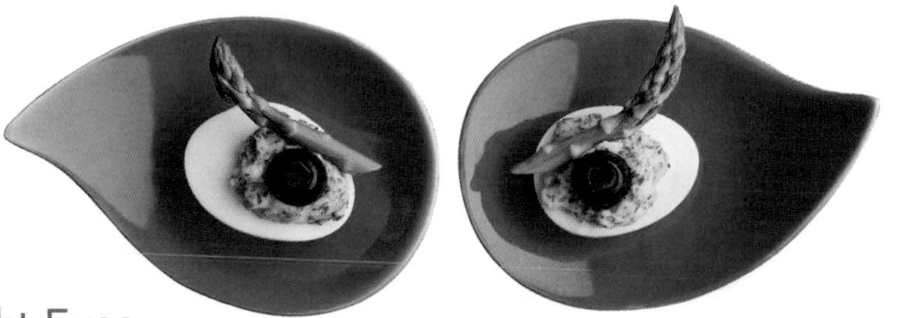

Night Eyes

INGREDIENTS

Parsley, finely chopped
Deviled egg mixture
Cooked egg whites
Red pepper
1 black olive and
2 asparagus tips
OR
1 pimiento-stuffed green olive
and 2 cornichons (gherkins)

INSTRUCTIONS

Stir chopped parsley into your favorite deviled egg mixture to give it a green tint; fill the cooked egg whites.

Version 1 (*above*): Use black-olive slices for pupils. Push a bit of red pepper into the center to add an evil glint. Add asparagus tips for eyebrows.

Version 2 (*page 144*): Use green-olive halves for eyes and cornichons for eyelids.
Cut tiny triangles of red pepper for eyelashes.

Gremlins Rule!

INGREDIENTS

Margarita mix (tequila optional) or lemonade
Grenadine
Skewer
1 each kiwi, lemon, lime, and orange
Maraschino cherry with stem
Toothpicks

INSTRUCTIONS

Serve chilled margarita mix on the rocks and add a splash of grenadine to add fun red color. Skewer a slice of kiwi for the face.

Cut a cherry in half and attach with pieces of toothpick for eyes.

Slip the skewer into the beverage glass. Add the cherry stem for a smile and twists of lemon, lime, and orange peel for hair.

Jack-o'-Lantern Cheese Balls

Make your favorite cream cheese ball recipe; shape the mixture into one large ball and one small ball. Roll each ball in crushed nacho cheese–flavored snack chips to cover completely. Place the cheese balls on a kale-lined platter. Cut pitted ripe olives into triangle-shape pieces. Press olive pieces into each cheese ball, making eyes and a mouth (you may need to remove chips from those areas to help the olives stick). Place a dill pickle half on the top of each cheese ball for a stem. Serve with crackers or chips.

Ghouls Just Wanna Have Fun

INGREDIENTS

- Large marshmallows
- Purchased fondant
- Black decorating gel
- Food coloring (optional)
- Small candies and decorating frosting (optional)
- Garlic press (optional)
- Pretzels (optional)

INSTRUCTIONS

To make a tall white ghoul, use clean scissors to snip one end each from two large marshmallows. Press cut ends together to make one tall marshmallow. Roll white fondant to about ¼ inch thick. Cut out a 4½-inch-diameter fondant circle. Shape the fondant circle over the marshmallow stack. Add eyes and a mouth using black decorating gel.

To make colorful ghouls, tint portions of fondant with a small amount of food coloring in desired colors. If desired, add two colors of food coloring to a fondant portion and blend only until marbled. Work with small portions at a time because fondant dries quickly; keep fondant covered when not in use.

For the striped version, make small ropes of different colors of the fondant. Press the ropes together and roll out with a rolling pin. Finish as directed above. If desired, use small candies for features, attaching them with decorating frosting. For hair-raising fun, push fondant through a garlic press and use the result to top a ghoul. Insert pieces of broken pretzel into the ghouls for arms.

Wacky Witches

INGREDIENTS

- Shredded coconut
- Liquid food coloring
- 1 17-ounce frozen cheesecake
- Fudge-striped cookies
- 1 package semisweet chocolate chips
- Nonpareils in assorted sizes and candy sprinkles
- Lime sherbet
- Small candies
- Cashews

INSTRUCTIONS

For hair, tint coconut with red and yellow liquid food coloring.

Cut the cheesecake into 1-inch-wide wedges. Trim the curved edge of each wedge to make a straight line, creating a tall triangle. Along the edge of a cookie, make a straight cut to create a flat base for the hat brim. Place the bottom of the cookie against the cheesecake wedge, with the cut side down, to check the shape; trim the cookie as needed to make it fit for the hat brim. Set aside.

Melt semisweet chocolate chips. Dip the cheesecake into the melted chocolate. Before the chocolate sets, sprinkle with nonpareils and set the cookie hat brim in place.

Before serving, place the hat on a plate. Using a small scoop, form a ball of lime sherbet for the head. Place the head against the hat brim and decorate the face with small candies for eyes, sprinkles for brows and mouth, and half a cashew for the nose. Press coconut in place for hair. Return to the freezer until serving time. Make additional witches.

Tombstone Trio

INGREDIENTS

- Large marshmallows
- White baking chocolate, melted
- Thick pretzel sticks
- Chocolate frosting
- Chocolate graham crackers
- Coconut
- Green food coloring
- Chocolate-filled butter cookies

INSTRUCTIONS

For each skeleton, cut a large marshmallow in half forming two rounds. Dip half the marshmallow rounds into melted white baking chocolate; place on a baking sheet lined with waxed paper. Dip thick pretzel stick pieces into melted white chocolate. If necessary, break pretzel pieces to make them the right lengths for shoulders, arms, and legs. Place on the lined baking sheet. Chill until set.

Using a pastry bag fitted with a small round tip, pipe chocolate frosting onto dipped marshmallow halves to make skeleton faces.

Attach a marshmallow skeleton head to a chocolate graham cracker using piped frosting. Pipe a small amount of frosting lengthwise onto the undersides of coated pretzel pieces, attaching them to the graham cracker to create a skeleton body. Use some melted white baking chocolate to pipe ribs onto the skeleton across the spine.

Tint coconut using green food coloring. Line a serving platter with green-tinted coconut "grass." Crush chocolate graham crackers and sprinkle on as "dirt."

Place the remaining marshmallow halves partly underneath and along the top of the skeleton-topped graham crackers to prop up the "graves." Arrange the skeletons on the "dirt" on the serving platter.

Using chocolate frosting, pipe desired sayings on chocolate-filled butter cookies to decorate as

tombstones. Use the marshmallow halves under the skeleton-topped graham crackers to support the cookies. Stick a decorated cookie into each marshmallow half, positioning it as a tombstone.

Spooky Stew

Spoon your favorite hot stew into individual serving dishes, filling each about two-thirds full. Using a pastry bag fitted with a large, plain round tip, pipe hot mashed potatoes into a ghost shape on top of each. Place capers for ghost eyes. Sprinkle shredded cheddar cheese around the base of each ghost and serve.

delicious DISGUISES

Clever (and hauntingly simple) decorating ideas put sweet and savory nibbles in the Halloween spirit.

WRITTEN BY **CAITLIN BERENS**
PHOTOGRAPHY BY **MARTY BALDWIN**

freaky frankencakes
Tinted with green aerosol icing, a fluffy marshmallow begins its transformation into a little monster, *opposite*. Black icing and pretzel sticks for bolts bring the cupcake topper to life.

eyes-on-you bites
The eyes have it with these haunting cakes, *top*. Make a red velvet cake mix and bake in fluted individual tube pans. Once the cakes have cooled, pipe white icing in a zigzag pattern around eyeball candies, making them the focal points.

sweetly mummified
Guests will get wrapped up in mummy-inspired chocolate cupcakes, *above left*. Pipe white frosting into random strips across a cupcake. Dots of red and black frosting form the penetrating eyes.

furry fun monsters
Icing tubes fitted with a multi-opening tip scare up a good time on these cupcakes, *above*. For the finishing touch, pipe white frosting for the eyes, adding dots of black icing to perfect a piercing glare.

edible still life

Elevate easy-does-it stove-top cookies into an artful display, *above*. Place the gooey mounds on a cake stand, then set a scene with store-bought marshmallow ghosts, pumpkins, and other seasonal treats.

bloodshot eyeballs

Turn your favorite peanut-butter-ball recipe into imitated eyeballs, *right*. Simply dip candies in white chocolate instead of milk chocolate, then use a small paintbrush and red food coloring to paint veins. Pipe small dots of black icing for pupils.

haunted hooting owl

Who-oo dares to eat this menacing owl? Everyone! Dip large pretzels in melted confectioner's coating, and layer sandwich cookies, white candies, and chocolate chips for wide-open eyes, *opposite*. Bits of black licorice attached with leftover candy coating form wistful eyebrows. Black sugar, a jelly bean, and small pieces of licorice candy complete the high-flying treat.

Scare up sweets that
show off in spooky disguises.
After all, Halloween is meant
for having wicked-good fun.
Who can resist a tasty
eyeball or two?

breadstick skeleton. Transform ready-to-bake breadsticks into bones for an appetizing skeleton, *this photo*. Simply snip the ends of the breadsticks before popping them into the oven. Arrange the bites around a marinara-sauce head, using mozzarella cheese and olives for the face.

pumpkin pick-me-up

This seasonal hummus pumpkin, *left*, is just begging to be carved into. Scoop hummus onto a serving plate; cover with finely shredded carrots. A small piece of green onion doubles as the perfect pumpkin stem.

biting bagel

Sink your teeth into this well-clad Transylvanian, *above*. Spread cream cheese on a mini bagel half, then add triangular strips of red pepper for a colorful bow tie. Olive pieces serve as the count's eyebrows and 'do, while a strip of carrot makes a wicked nose. Close the casket on this treat with capers for eyes and thin slices of green onion for the mouth.

menacing stare

You're sure to relish this vegetable ensemble, *left*. Pit avocado halves and brush them with lemon juice, then fill the centers with cocktail sauce. Small mozzarella balls topped with olives and bits of pimiento serve as the eyeballs. Embed them in strips of roasted red pepper. Thinly sliced radishes finish the chilling treat.

FOOD STYLED BY **GREG LUNA & DIANNA NOLIN**
PHOTOGRAPHY BY **MARTY BALDWIN**

creature TREATS

These creepy crawlers, spooky cats, and kooky creatures are ready to thrill, chill—and be savored!

"hairry" the scary spider
Beware, arachnophobes. This furry spider's fangs are oh so sweet! The treat starts as a cake baked in a bowl and slathered with frosting, *this photo*. Crème-filled rolled wafers give "Hairry" his lanky legs, candies give him googly eyes, and chocolate curls make him fearfully furry ... in a cute way.

nutty owl

As if a delicious cheese ball weren't treat enough, this Halloween snack goes out on a (breadstick) limb as a finely feathered owl, *this photo*. Apple slices, nuts, and capers give this bird its ruffled character.

not-so-creepy alley cat pop
Partygoers won't care one bit if this black cat crosses their paths—especially when the feline is a rice cereal bar in delicious chocolate disguise. Superstitious? Melted butterscotch chips turn black cats into less-scary calico kitties, *this photo*. Candy trims make this crazed cat as scary or spooky as you like.

batty bites

Will your guests take flight—or a bite—when they see these freaky fliers? Chocolate-dipped toaster pastries make tasty wings, while chocolate-covered sandwich cookies fill the role of the bats' bodies, *this photo*. Colorful decorative sprinkles make the clever creatures silly rather than sinister.

cockeyed cuckoos

Looking to scare up some laughs? These silly birds will get the giggles going! Start with meatballs and marinara sauce atop ciabatta rolls, and add a little hocus-pocus here and there: cream-cheese balls dotted with olive pieces for the eyes, sweet peppers for the beak and brows, plus snipped chives and shredded carrots to top off our featherbrained friends.

Alley Cat Pops

INGREDIENTS

- Peanut- or marshmallow-flavored cereal bars
- Semisweet chocolate, melted
- Butterscotch-flavored pieces, melted
- Candy-coated milk chocolate pieces
- Confetti sprinkles
- White baking pieces, melted

INSTRUCTIONS

Insert a frozen-treat stick into the end of each cereal bar rectangle. Brush tops and sides of each bar with semisweet chocolate; place coated bars on a baking sheet lined with waxed paper. Let stand until chocolate is set.

For ears, cut triangle shapes from heavy-duty foil. Brush melted chocolate onto one side of triangles; place on a baking sheet lined with waxed paper. Chill until chocolate is set. Brush bars with melted butterscotch to make spots on chocolate-covered bars. Use melted chocolate to attach candy-coated milk chocolate pieces for eyes and a confetti sprinkle for the nose. Pipe melted white baking pieces on face for whiskers and a mouth.

Peel foil from chocolate ears and use melted chocolate to attach ears to the backs of the cat pops. Chill to set.

Batty Bites

For a large bat, cut a chocolate-flavored breakfast pastry in half diagonally. For a small bat, cut a chocolate-flavored breakfast pastry in half diagonally and then in half again, making four triangles.

To make a bat, carefully dip one side of each of two pastry triangles into melted semisweet chocolate. Place triangles, chocolate sides up, on a baking sheet lined with waxed paper. Embellish the wings with decorative sprinkles.

Dip a cream-filled chocolate sandwich cookie (large for a large bat or miniature for a small bat) into melted chocolate. Place a cookie body on top of the triangle wings. Add eyes of almond slices, sunflower kernels, or pumpkin seeds. For the almond eyes, use miniature chocolate pieces as pupils. Chill until chocolate is set.

Scary Spider Cake

INGREDIENTS

- 1 one-layer cake mix, any flavor
- 8 crème-filled rolled wafer cookies
- Semisweet chocolate, melted
- Chocolate frosting
- White licorice candies
- White pastel wafer candies
- Candy-coated milk chocolate pieces
- Red licorice candy
- Milk chocolate, grated

INSTRUCTIONS

Prepare and bake a one-layer cake according to package instructions, except pour batter into a greased and floured 1½-quart ovenproof glass bowl. Bake for 35 to 40 minutes or until a toothpick inserted near center comes out clean. Let cake cool for 5 minutes. Remove from bowl and cool completely on a wire rack.

Cut wafer cookies in half at a slight angle. Dip the angled ends of each cookie into melted semisweet chocolate; place each cookie, with two dipped ends together to form a leg, on a baking sheet lined with waxed paper. Chill until chocolate is set.

Frost rounded surface of cake with chocolate frosting. Add white licorice candies to make a mouth. Press on pastel wafer candies as eyes. Use frosting to attach candy-coated milk chocolate pieces as pupils. Cut two corners from red licorice candy; use pointy corners as fangs. Top cake with curly grated milk chocolate. Insert cookie legs into each side of cake.

Cockeyed Cuckoos

For each sandwich, spoon two hot marinara-coated meatballs on top of a split and toasted roll. Roll two small pieces of cream cheese into separate balls.

Gently push a cream cheese ball into the front of each meatball, making an eye. Cut pitted ripe olives into small pieces; press into the front of each cream cheese ball as a pupil. Cut orange and/or yellow sweet peppers into pieces; arrange on meatballs as beaks and eyebrows. Arrange julienne carrots and/or chives on sandwiches to resemble feathers.

Nutty Owl

INGREDIENTS

- 2 8-ounce packages cream cheese
- 2 cups finely shredded smoked cheddar, Swiss, or Gouda
- ½ cup butter or margarine
- 2 tablespoons milk
- 2 teaspoons steak sauce
- 1 green apple
- 3 cashews
- Sliced almonds
- 2 capers
- Sprig of parsley
- 1 breadstick

INSTRUCTIONS

Let cream cheese, shredded cheese, and butter stand at room temperature for 30 minutes. Add milk and steak sauce; beat until fluffy. Cover and chill for 4 to 24 hours.

For each owl, shape about 2 tablespoons of the mixture into an oval body. Shape 2 rounded teaspoons into a ball for the head. Press the shapes together.

Cut six thin apple slices in assorted sizes for wings, and press into the sides of the body. Push two cashews into the body for feet and one cashew into the head for the beak. Cover the body with almond slices. Add caper eyes, and arrange almond slices and a sprig of parsley on the head. Place a breadstick for the tree branch.

Miller's
DEAD &
BREAKFAST
Inn
Est. 2010
vacancy

Sleeping
Like the
DEAD

outdoor decor

Raise spirits and send chills down spines with seasonal settings that creep along the front lawn, scamper up the house, and set up camp on the porch. These beguiling characters might startle, but trick-or-treaters and neighbors will all be entranced.

skeleton crew

Greet trick-or-treaters with a troupe of frolicking skeletons dressed for Halloween fun. Prop, brace, or hang the frisky figures in your front yard to add bone-chilling excitement.

PRODUCED BY **SHAWN ROORDA**
WRITTEN BY **DEBRA WITTRUP**
PHOTOGRAPHY BY **JASON DONNELLY**

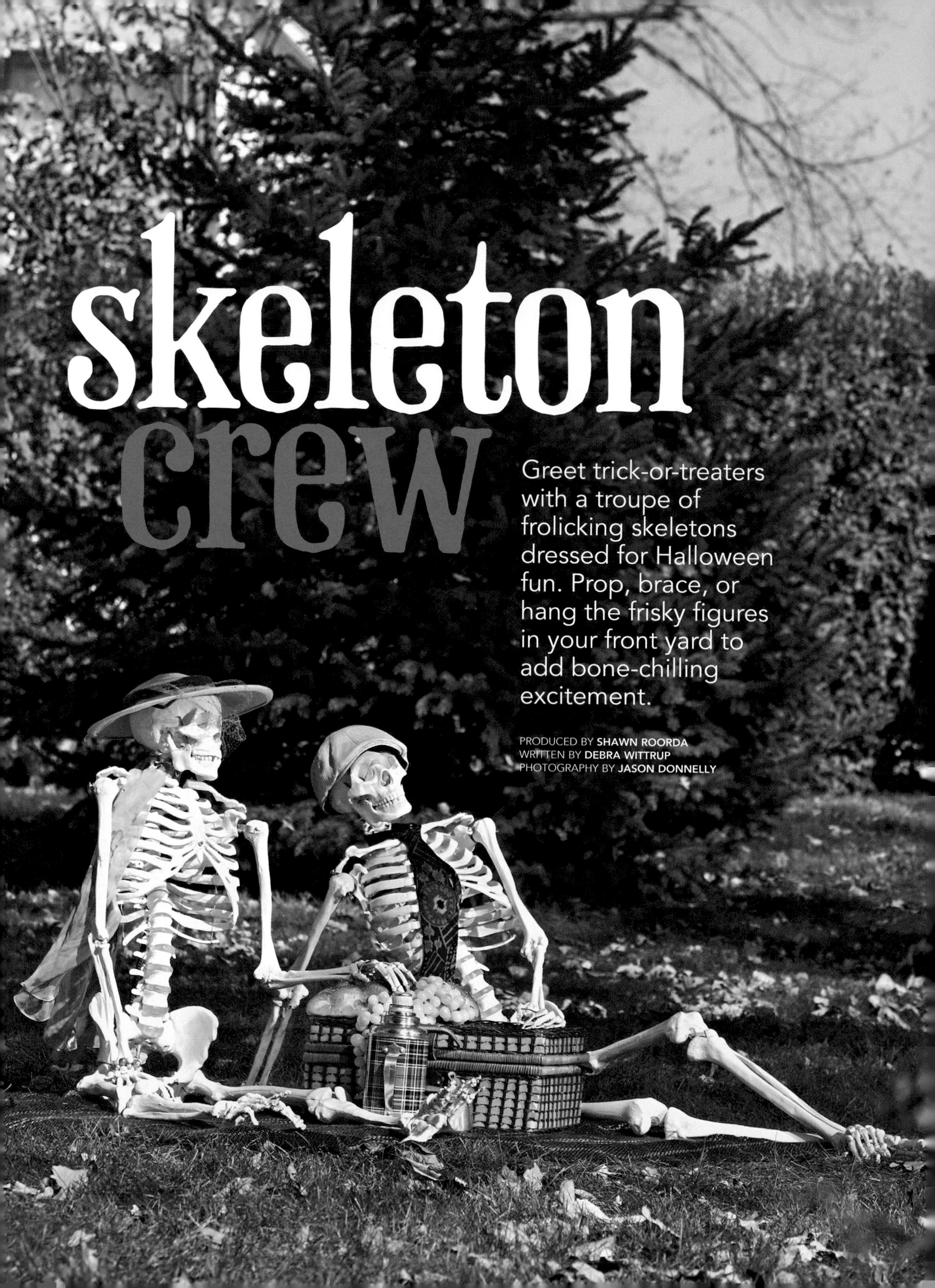

picnic in perpetuity
Cater a picnic for the graveyard shift. Dolled up for their outing in hats, scarf, and tie, our perpetual picnickers, *opposite*, are propped up with rebar stakes pushed into the ground. Spread a blanket, and top it with a woven basket, faux fruit, and an insulated bottle. Weight the bottle with pebbles inside, and use ground stakes to hold the blanket in place. If you want this sociable vignette to last, use weather-resistant props.

climb time
These guys, *right*, don't need to worry about pulled muscles as they caper from porch to rooftop. Easy to pose and to secure with nearly invisible fishing line, the plastic skeletons can withstand the weather and hang out for the entire season. How you hang or pose your figures will depend on what types of skeletons you have. Be prepared to improvise!

past her prime

Some hostesses love handing out treats so much that they can't give it up—even after they've passed on. This skeleton on a stand, *opposite*, makes a spirited first impression at the front door. Her posable arms provide the brace for a sweets-laden tray hot-glued to her hands. Dressed in a skirt, apron, and pearls, she's perfectly attired to greet guests.

bad to the bone

Caught climbing trees and burrowing in the leaf pile, these scampering skeletons, *right*, prove you're never too old for pranks. A variety of skeleton types are available online—some pose, some stand, some bend. Choose the type that meets your needs. These bad boys are basic plastic articulated figures secured in place with fishing line to wreak merry mayhem.

in fine form

Create the petrified poses of croquet-playing skeletons, *opposite*, by using fishing line to tie each player to a long stake pushed into the ground. Tie the croquet mallets to the skeletons with fishing line. Kicked back with a cool glass of lemonade, the jointed old duffer watching the action from the wooden lawn chair is simply propped in place.

rest your bones

It looks as if these chaps, *above*, may have been waiting too long for their dates to arrive! Dressed in simple finery with top hats, silky bow ties, and red boutonnieres, the eerie ensemble of skeletal swains has more impact than a single figure would. It's a snap to prop up our ethereal escorts with lengths of rebar pushed through their rib cages and into the ground.

As trick-or-treaters head your way at sundown, follow our instructions to greet them with your own creatures of the night.

DESIGNED BY **SCOTT SMITH**
WRITTEN BY **BEVERLY RIVERS**
PHOTOGRAPHY BY **BLAINE MOATS** AND **JAY WILDE**

LIVELY SHADOWS

mice and men

With the help of plywood and paint, your yard will be crawling with creepy cutouts. Glow-in-the-dark paint and LED bulbs bring them to life after dark. Keeping this bony gent upright is as easy as making a quick cauldron of spider stew. Just attach a piece of PVC pipe to his back and push it into the ground—he won't be going anywhere!

Feeling a little superstitious? Black cats cross every path in this yard. But there's no bad luck here—just lots of fun and excitement.

'fraidy cats

Greet little goblins and their mummies and daddies with eerie smiles and haunting eyes. These jack-o'-lanterns light up the pathway to the door with their yellow cellophane features, which are enhanced by a hidden spotlight. Keep them company with black cat cutouts—eyes lit and ready to pounce.

lamppost illusion

Strange things occur at dusk when Halloween nears. Cast a light on the goings-on with a temporary lamppost. Cut your own post from plywood, give it a coat of exterior paint, and attach a garden-variety candle lantern with a large hook. The little ghouls will thank you for the warm glow.

witch way?
Line your driveway and sidewalk with spooktacular figures cut from plywood and painted black. This fearsome duo gives out sweet offerings instead of scary vibes. Make your own colorful goody bucket. All you need is a metal paint can, peel-and-stick crafts foam, and scissors.

Lively Shadows

MATERIALS

1-inch-thick plywood
Jigsaw
Drill
Gray or black exterior primer
Black flat exterior paint
Glow-in-the-dark paint
Paintbrushes
Needle-nose pliers
LED battery-operated candle lights
Silver or black duct tape
Yellow cellophane
Outdoor spotlight
PVC pipe
Metal pipe straps with screws
6-inch-long screws
Garden lantern with hook
Battery-operated pillar candle

INSTRUCTIONS

To create cutouts, refer to our patterns, *pages 180–181*, for guidance. Or photocopy the patterns and transfer the images in desired size onto 1-inch plywood.

Trace or draw the shapes on the plywood in desired size. Using a jigsaw, cut out the shapes. For cat and rat eyes, drill holes large enough to accommodate an LED bulb.

For features on the ghost, skeleton, and jack-o'-lanterns, drill a large hole into the middle of each space outlined for eyes, noses, or mouths. Then insert the blade of your jigsaw and cut out the shape.

Paint all cutouts with primer and let dry. Paint all cutouts with black paint. Let dry thoroughly.

Referring to the pattern for guidance, draw the skeleton and tombstone details with a pencil. With a small brush, apply glow-in-the-dark paint to the penciled lines. Let the paint dry.

For the lights in the eyes, use needle-nose pliers to remove and discard the candle tip from each LED bulb (see photo A). Insert the bulb into the eyehole in the cutout, and then tape over the back of the LED light to secure (see photo B).

To light the jack-o'-lantern, cover the backs of the cutout features with yellow cellophane; tape in place. Position an outdoor spotlight behind the cutout.

To secure larger cutouts to the ground, attach a length of PVC pipe to the back of the cutout (see photo C), allowing at least 12 inches to extend below the bottom of the shape. Use pipe straps and screws to secure the pipe to the cutout. Paint pipe and straps black. Tap the pipe into the ground using a hammer or mallet.

To secure the rats and cats to the ground, screw the first 1½ inches of 6-inch-long screws into the bottoms of the feet; push or tap the screws into the ground.

For the light on the lamppost, securely attach a garden lantern to the cutout, then place a battery-operated pillar candle inside.

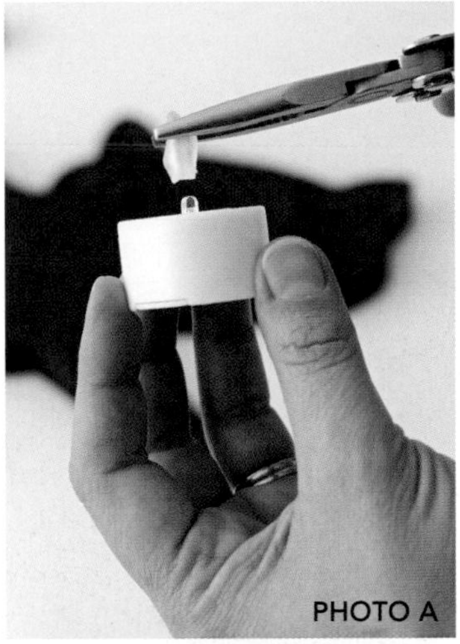
PHOTO A

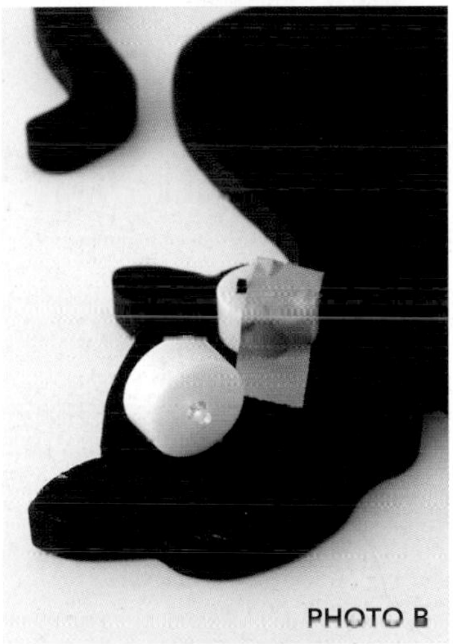
PHOTO B

PHOTO C

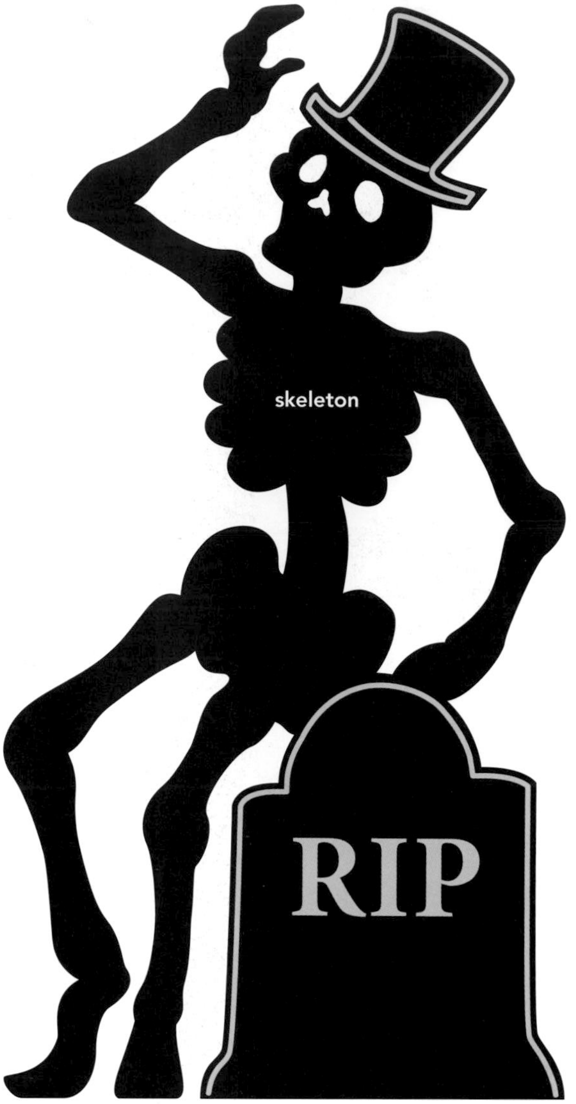
skeleton
RIP

rats

pumpkins

ghost

cat

witch

lamppost

THE DEAD AND BREAKFAST INN

Where can a ghoul go to rest her tired bones?
To a "dead and breakfast," of course, where the guests expired long before their welcome ever did.
Here's how—with a little ingenuity—you can transform your front yard into an enchanted ever-after.

WRITTEN AND PRODUCED BY **KATHY BARNES** PHOTOGRAPHY BY **CAMERON SADEGHPOUR**

final resting place
This old soul has been waiting a frighteningly long time for room service. Create a comfy spot for spirits to relax using secondhand odds and ends arranged to look like a hotel suite. Instructions for the sign are on *page 188*.

guest arrival
A bony bride and her drawn husband, *above left*, plan to spend a very long honeymoon here.

a simple promise
For this couple, the honeymoon phase may never end. Give wedding vows a whole new meaning with a timeless wish painted on a weathered wood sign, *above*. Get the instructions on *page 188*.

turndown service
Make this boo-doir, *left*, by pounding a rusty iron head- and footboard into the ground. Tea stain gives a centuries-old look to a pair of plain white pillowcases. Write the words on the cases with a permanent marker.

haunted hotel
There's always room for more ghoulish guests. A cast-off post gets a new life when paired with a do-it-yourself sign, *this photo*. Be sure your welcome sign reads "vacancy" so trick-or-treaters will know they can approach. Instructions are on *page 188*.

sit a spell
Black spray paint brings together a mishmash of inexpensive tableware, including flatware, plates, and candlesticks, *this photo*. Find bridal attire—an ideal shade of ghostly white—at a thrift store.

rest in peace

Assemble this bed, *above*, by screwing a cleat into a cast-off headboard and footboard. The cleat creates a ledge for a sheet of clear acrylic—the perfect spooky resting place for a levitating skeleton.

dead tired

Puns and wordplay on signs made from a salvaged board, *right*, take the edge off the scare factor. See the instructions on *page 188*.

check-in time

Position your concierge (a Halloween-store mannequin), *far right*, near the front door to greet guests. He warns visitors of a quiet stay: There are no activities planned, and once you check in, you'll never leave. Instructions are on *page 188*.

Inn Signboard

MATERIALS

1×8 boards
1×2 backing boards
Six ½-inch wood screws
Latex paint: gray, dark brown, and white
Two 2-inch-wide paintbrushes
Tracing paper and pencil
Graphite transfer paper
Artist's liner brush
Acrylic crafts paint: black
Eye screws and chain
Post

INSTRUCTIONS

Cut sign pieces, two backing boards, and vacancy sign to size, referring to pattern dimensions, *opposite.* Assemble sign by screwing horizontal backing boards to the back of sign pieces.

Mix a 1:1 solution of water and gray or dark brown paint to create a color wash. Dip a brush into the wash, wiping off the excess. Drag the brush lightly across the wood surface to give it an aged look. (Let texture of the wood show.) Allow it to dry for 5 minutes. Pick up a scant amount of white paint on a second brush. Dry-brush white paint where you want the lightest areas; let dry. Repeat with dark brown around the edges of the boards; let dry.

Photocopy the patterns (or download and print them) in desired size; trace designs onto tracing paper to make it easier to place the design. Transfer patterns to the sign using graphite transfer paper. Use a pencil to darken the graphite lines if necessary.

Use a liner brush and black acrylic paint to paint the lettering onto the boards. Let the paint dry.

Insert eye screws and attach chains for hanging the sign. Hang from the post.

Small Signs

MATERIALS

Aged barn boards
Latex paint: gray, dark brown, and white
Two 2-inch-wide paintbrushes
Tracing paper and pencil
Graphite transfer paper
Artist's liner brush
Acrylic crafts paint: black
Barbed wire or eye screws

INSTRUCTIONS

Gather miscellaneous pieces of aged board and cut to size, referring to the pattern dimensions, *opposite* and *page 190.* Drill hanging holes if desired.

Referring to the inn signboard instructions, *left,* transfer patterns, then paint, and hang the signs using barbed wire or eye screws.

Check-In Card

MATERIALS

Cardstock: red and white
Crafts glue
Black butler's tray
Concierge bell

INSTRUCTIONS

Photocopy the "Check in Here" pattern, *page 190* (or download and print it), onto white cardstock; cut the cardstock into a square. Cut an 8×16-inch piece of red cardstock. Fold the red cardstock in half. Glue the white message to the front half of the card with the fold at the top. Display on a butler's tray with a concierge bell.

Go to ***BHG.com/HTTbookinn*** for free printable patterns and instructions for all these projects.

Check in Here

... but you can't check out

sources

For more information, contact the listed sources. Most products used in the projects in this book are available at fabrics, crafts, and department stores. We cannot guarantee availability of items.

Pumpkin Pets on Parade

PAGES 22–27

Project designer—Matthew Mead, *matthewmeadstyle.com.*

Halloween Stars

PAGES 28–45

Location—Some projects photographed at The Garden Barn, *thegardenbarn.com.*

Welcome All Spirits

PAGES 50–65

Paper designer—Brandy Faulkner, *brandywine.etsy.com.* **Skeleton stamp** (for similar stamps): *goreydetails.net.* **Table base urns**—*homedepot.com.* **Flameless battery-operated candles**—*batteryoperatedcandles.net.* **Location**—Salisbury House, *salisburyhouse.org.*

Wicked-Easy Halloween Party

PAGES 66–79

Cookies and projects in partnership with Sweet Tooth Cottage—Kim M. Byers, The Celebration Shoppe, LLC, Sunbury, Ohio; 740/972-1688; *thecelebrationshoppe.com.*

Monster Bash

PAGES 80–95

Cupcake and brownie pop molds—Wilton, *wilton.com* (available at crafts stores). **Epson PictureMate photo printer**—Epson, *epson.com.*

Fright Night Invites

PAGES 96–103

Trick-or-treat bag invitation rub-on letters—Fancy Pants Designs, *fancypantsdesigns.com.* **Candy-pattern paper**—K&Company, *kandcompany.eksuccessbrands.com.* **Cat eye**—Creatology, *michaels.com.*

Ultimate Party Guide

PAGES 104–113

Favor bag: Die cuts (#655568 Phrase, Sweet Skull, and Top Hat)—Sizzix, *sizzix.com.* **Acrylic crafts paints**—Plaid Apple Barrel, *plaidonline.com* (available at crafts stores). **Candy corn centerpiece:** Foam paint—DecoArt, *decoart.com* (available at crafts stores). **Modeling compound**—Crayola Model Magic, *crayola.com* (available at crafts stores). **Glow-in-the-dark paint**—Plaid Glo Away, *plaidonline.com* (available at crafts stores). **Plastic-foam shapes**—FloraCraft (available at crafts stores). **For more ideas and projects,** go to *fiskars.com, kraftfood.com,* and *joann.com.*

When I Grow Up!

PAGES 126–133

Chef apron and hat—Growing Cooks, *growingcooks.com.* **Wool beret**—The Village Hat Shop, *villagehatshop.com.* **Plush wolf toy**—Stuffed Ark, *stuffedark.com.* **Skirt (Musical)**—Anna Bean, *annabean.com.* **Leotard, slippers, and tights**—Discount Dance Supply, *discountdance.com.*

All Decked Out

PAGES 134–141

Pirate chest and contents—Oriental Trading Co., *orientaltrading.com.*

Lively Shadows

PAGES 174–181

Acrylic green crafts paint—Plaid Apple Barrel Gloss Glow-in-the-Dark, *plaidonline.com* (available at crafts stores). **Flameless battery-operated candles**—*batteryoperatedcandles.net.*

The Dead and Breakfast Inn

PAGES 182–190

Location—Jordan House, *thejordanhouse.org.* **Horse**—Warren Johnson. **Skeletons**—*egeneralmedical.com.*

Published by:
Houghton Mifflin Harcourt
Boston • New York
www.hmhbooks.com

Library of Congress Control Number available from the publisher upon request.
ISBN: 978-1-118-43517-5 (pbk)

Printed in the United States of America

DOR 10 9 8 7 6 5 4 3 2 1

NOTE TO THE READERS: Due to differing conditions, tools, and individual skills, Houghton Mifflin Harcourt assumes no responsibility for any damages, injuries suffered, or losses incurred as a result of following the information published in this book. Before beginning any project, review the instructions carefully, and if any doubts or questions remain, consult local experts or authorities. Because codes and regulations vary greatly, you always should check with authorities to ensure that your project complies with all applicable local codes and regulations. Always read and observe all of the safety precautions provided by manufacturers of any tools, equipment, or supplies, and follow all accepted safety procedures.

BETTER HOMES AND GARDENS® MAGAZINE
Gayle Goodson Butler
Editor in Chief
Oma Blaise Ford
Executive Editor
Michael D. Belknap
Creative Director

BETTER HOMES AND GARDENS® BEST OF HALLOWEEN TRICKS & TREATS
Contributing Editor: **Kathleen Armentrout**
Contributing Designer: **Angie Hoogensen**
Contributing Copy Editor: **Nancy Dietz**

SPECIAL INTEREST MEDIA
Editorial Director: **James D. Blume**
Content Director, Home: **Jill Waage**
Deputy Content Director, Home: **Karman Hotchkiss**
Senior Holidays Editor: **Ann Blevins**
Managing Editor: **Doug Kouma**
Art Director: **Gene Rauch**
Group Editor: **Lacey Howard**
Assistant Managing Editor: **Jennifer Speer Ramundt**
Business Director: **Janice Croat**

MEREDITH NATIONAL MEDIA GROUP
President: **Tom Harty**
Executive Vice President: **Doug Olson**

MEREDITH CORPORATION
Chairman and Chief Executive Officer: **Stephen M. Lacy**

HOUGHTON MIFFLIN HARCOURT
Vice President and Publisher: **Natalie Chapman**
Editorial Director: **Cindy Kitchel**
Acquisitions Editor: **Pam Mourouzis**
Production Director: **Diana Cisek**
Production Manager: **John Simko**